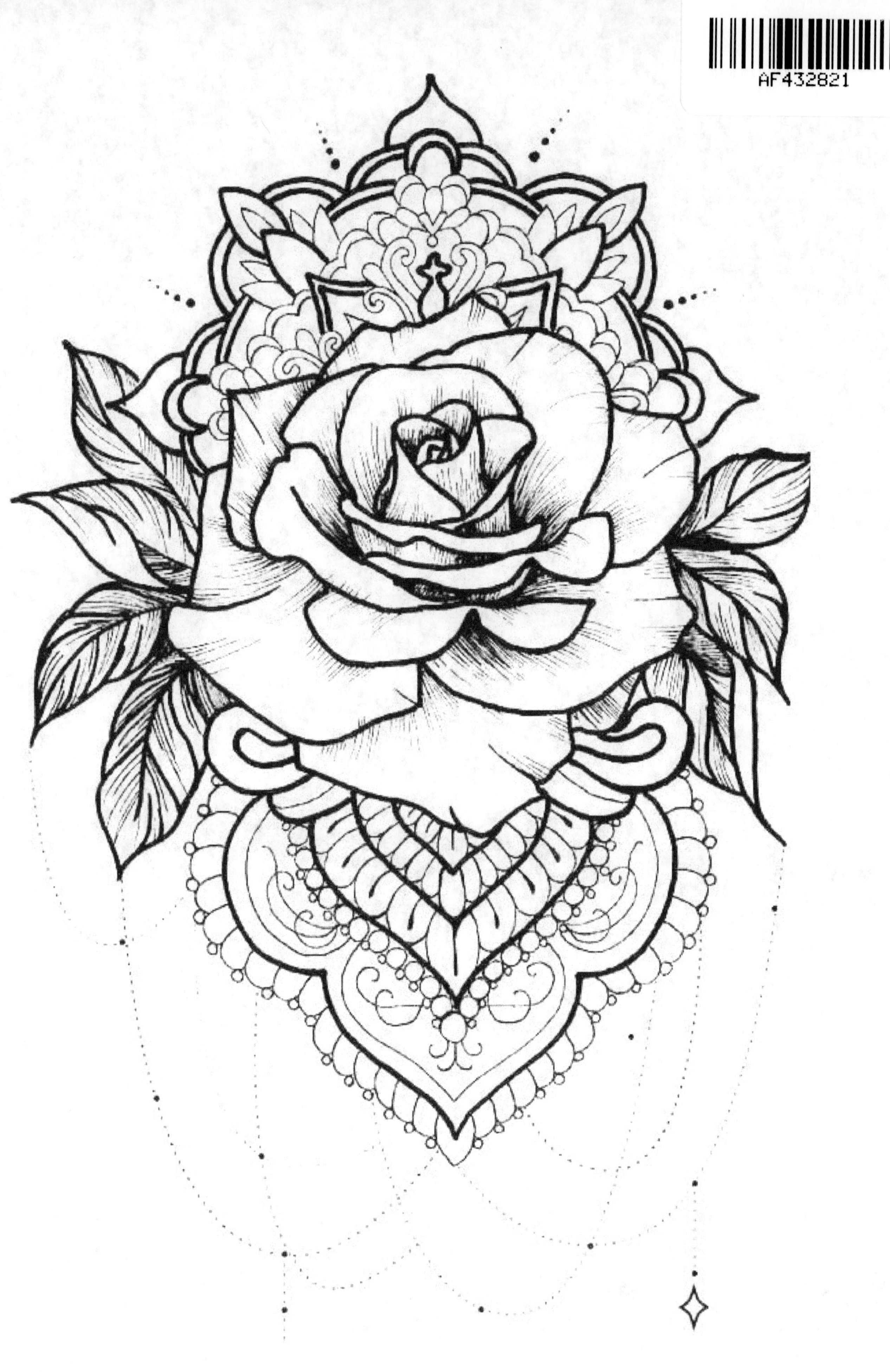
AF432821

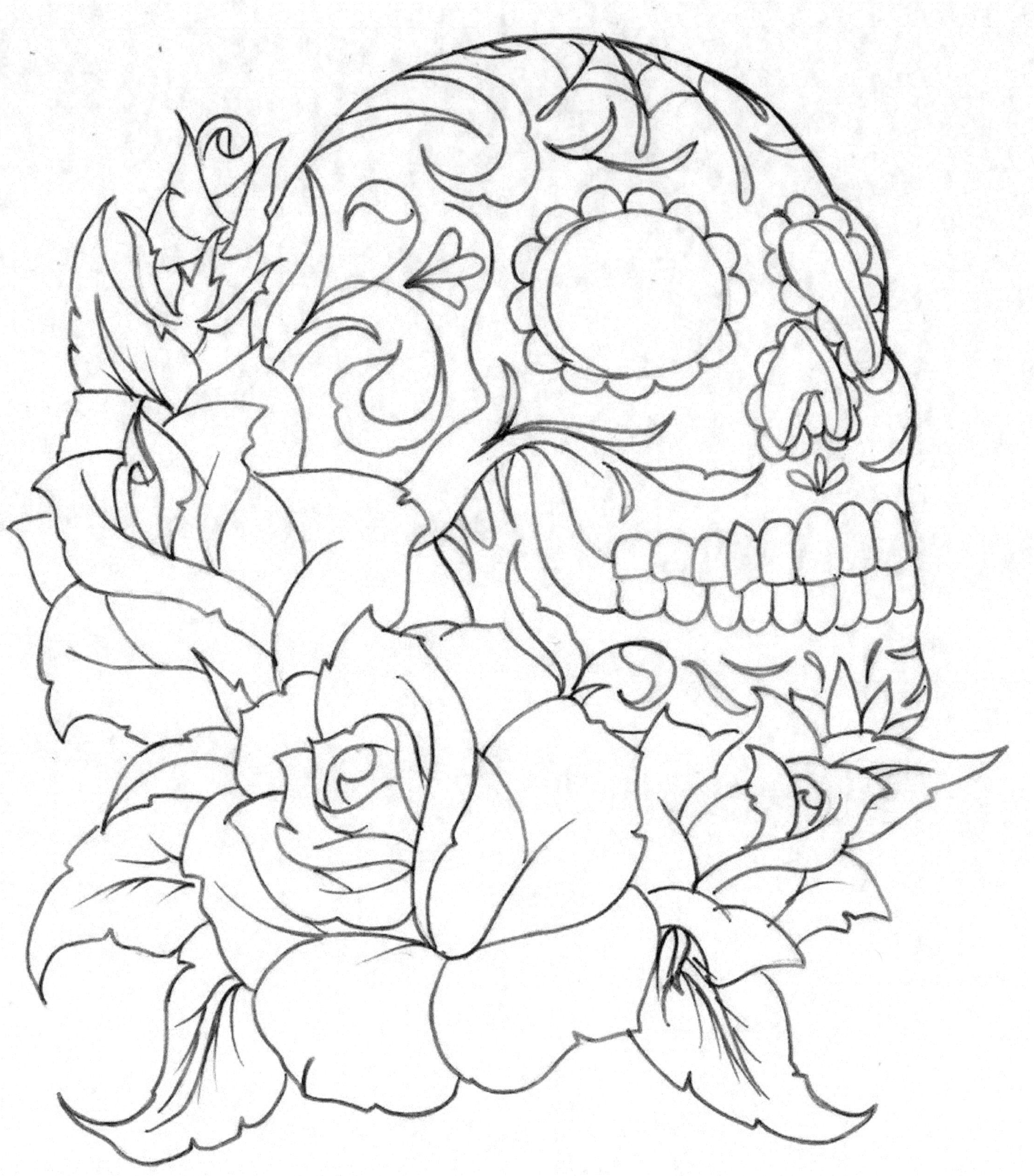

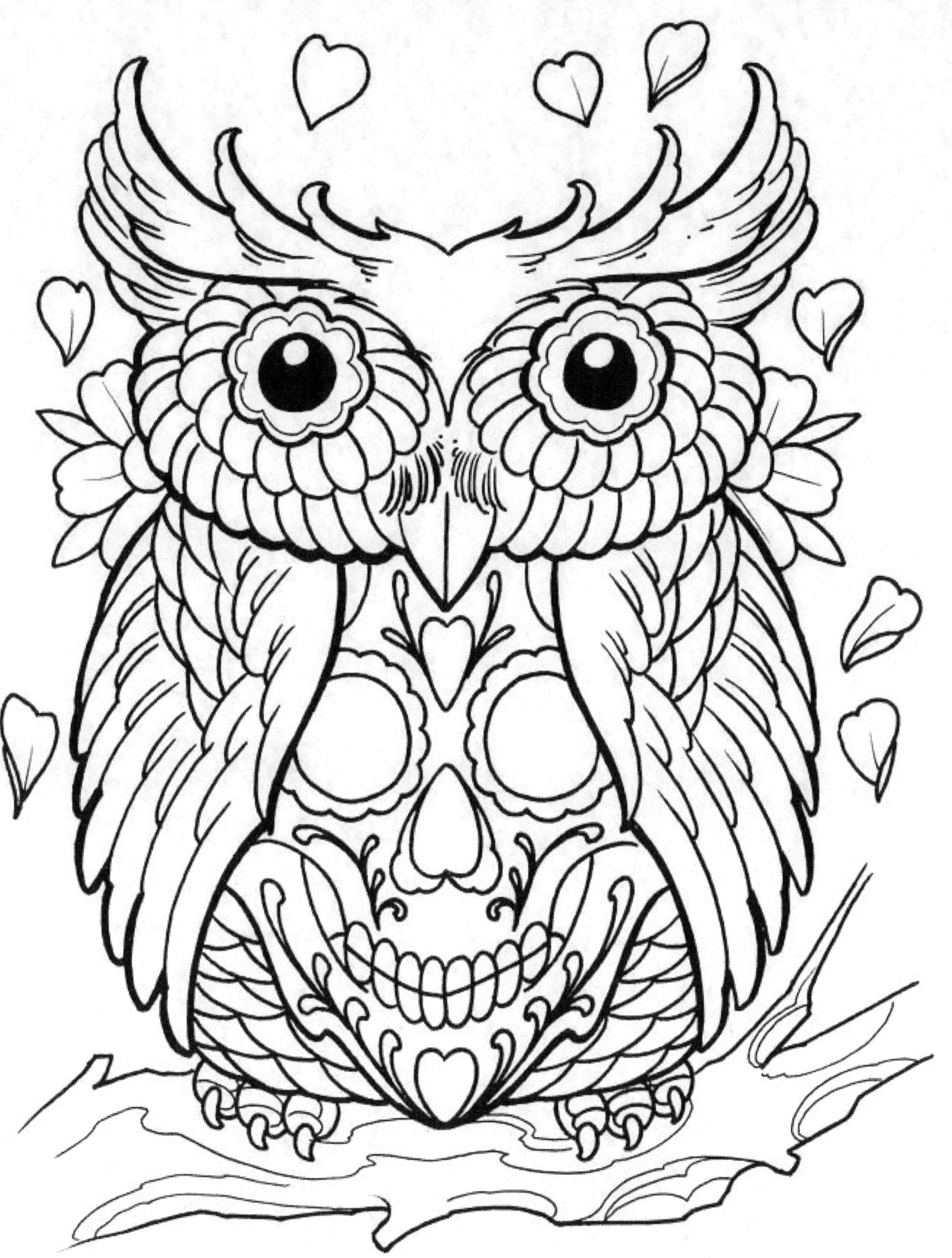

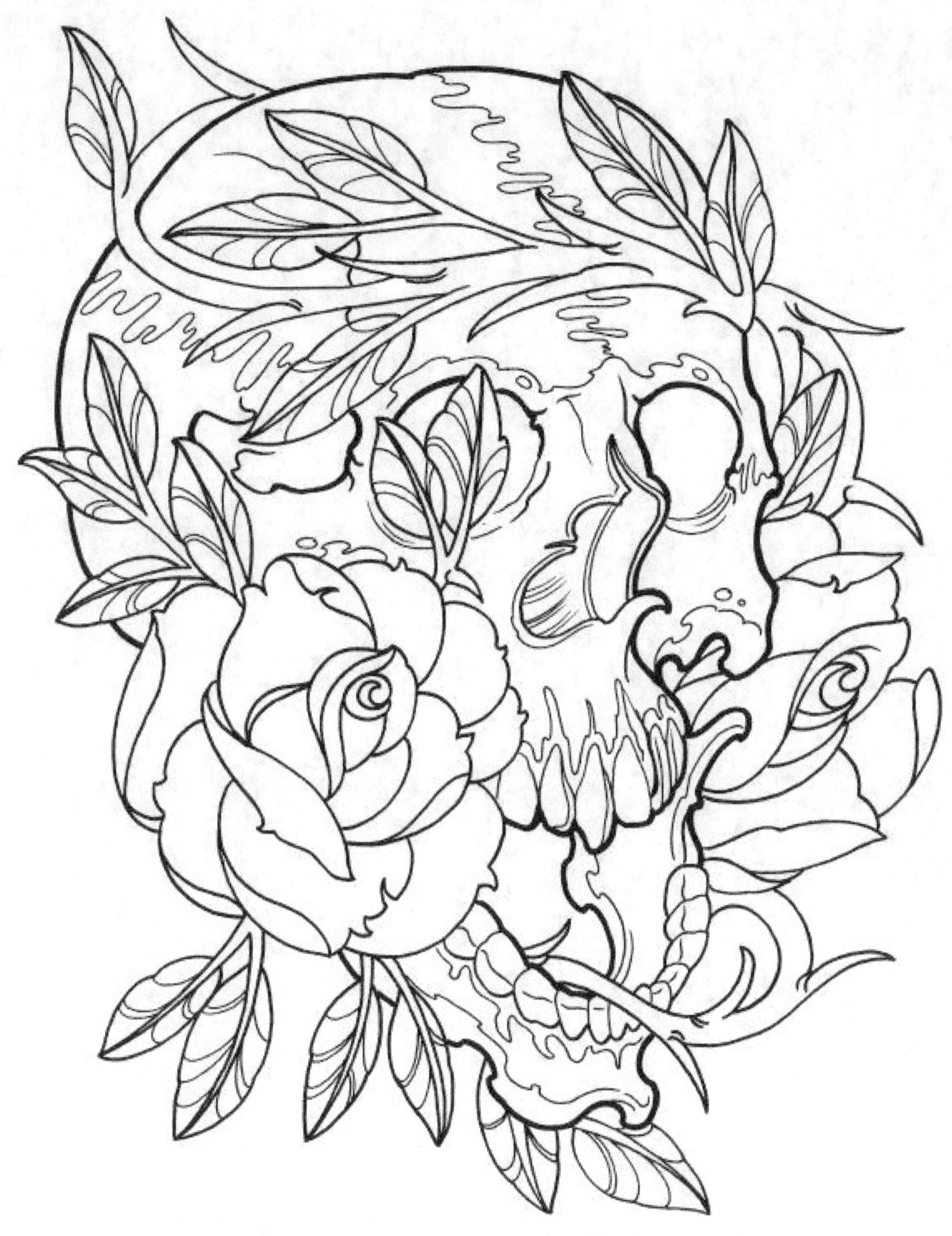

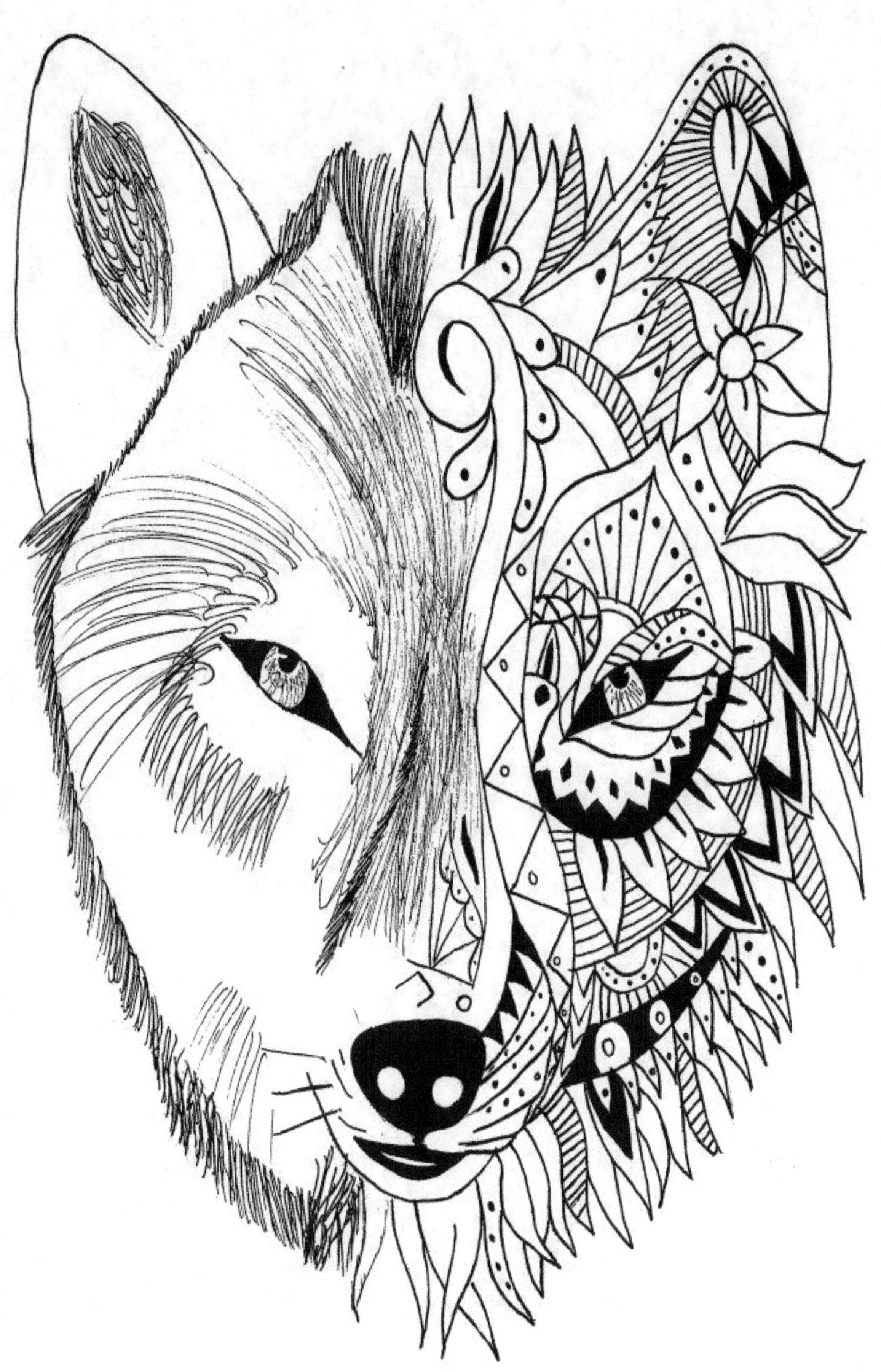

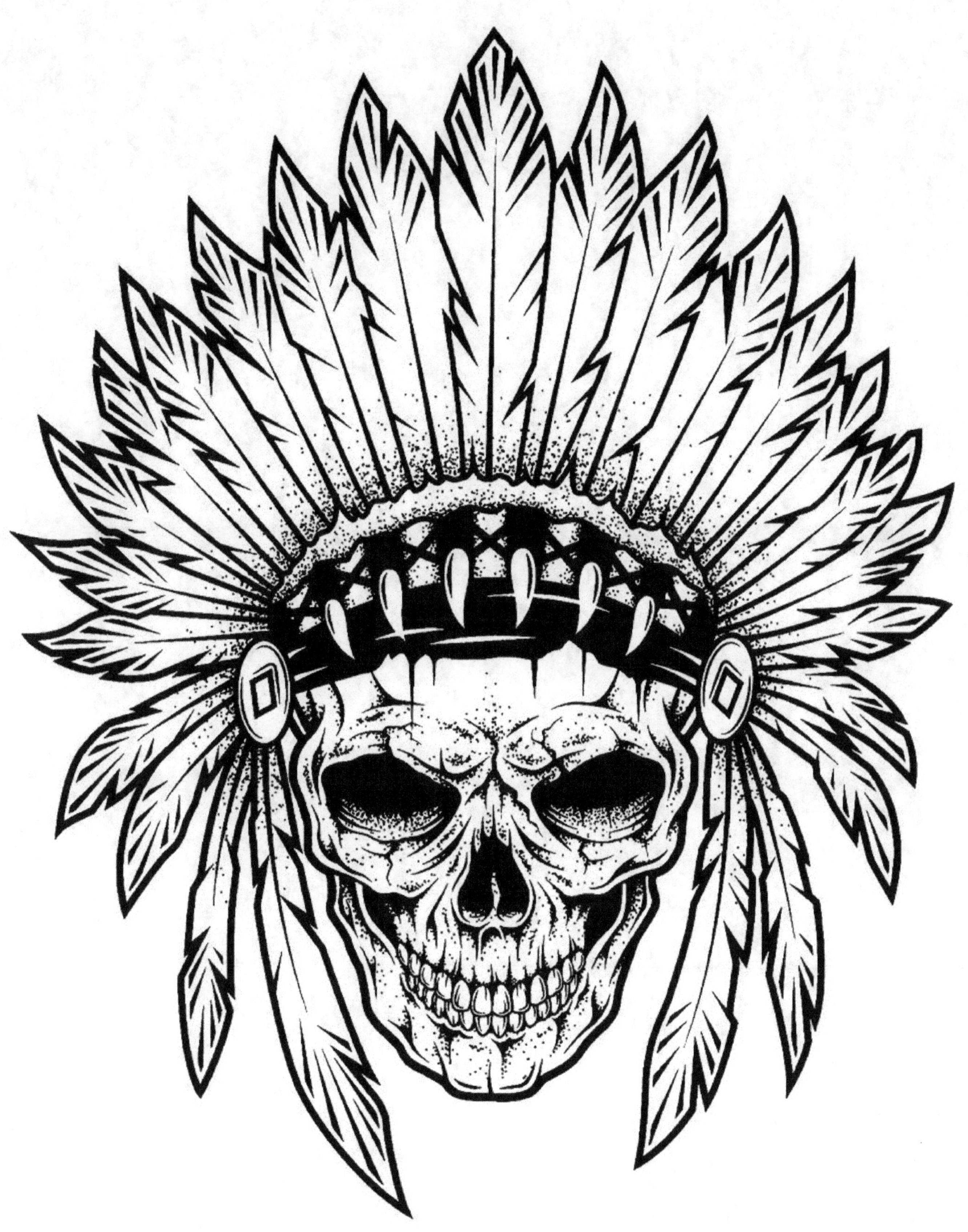

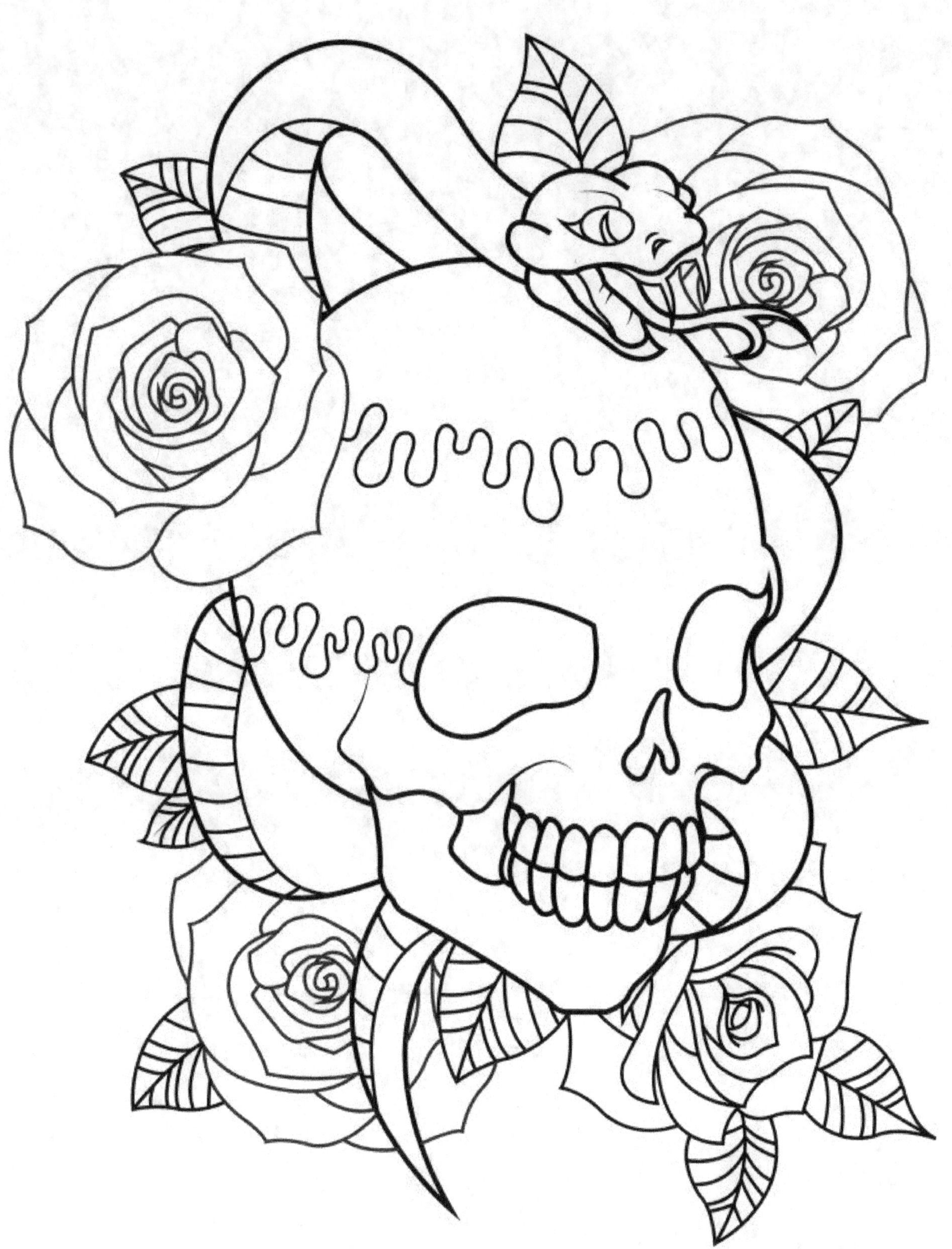

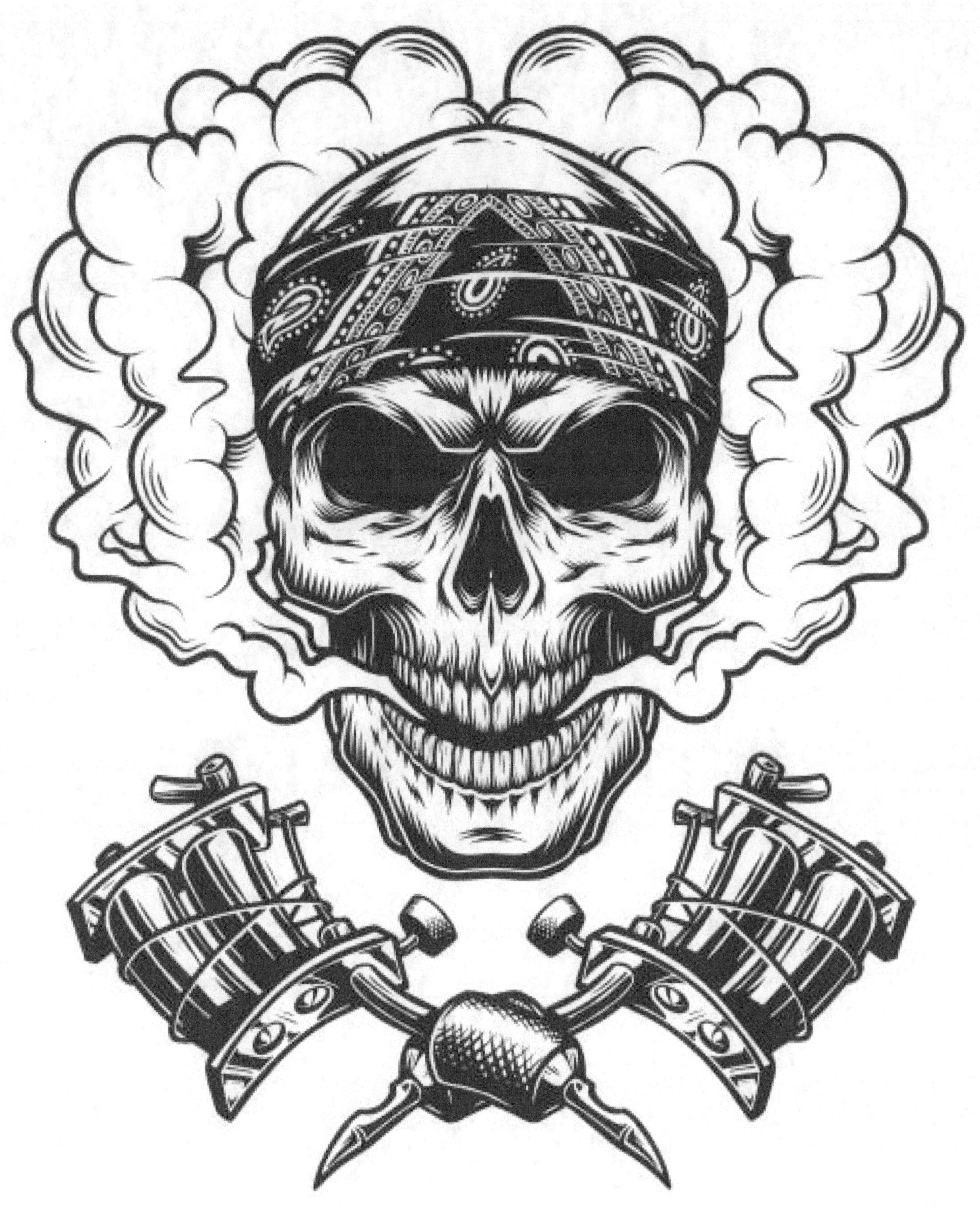

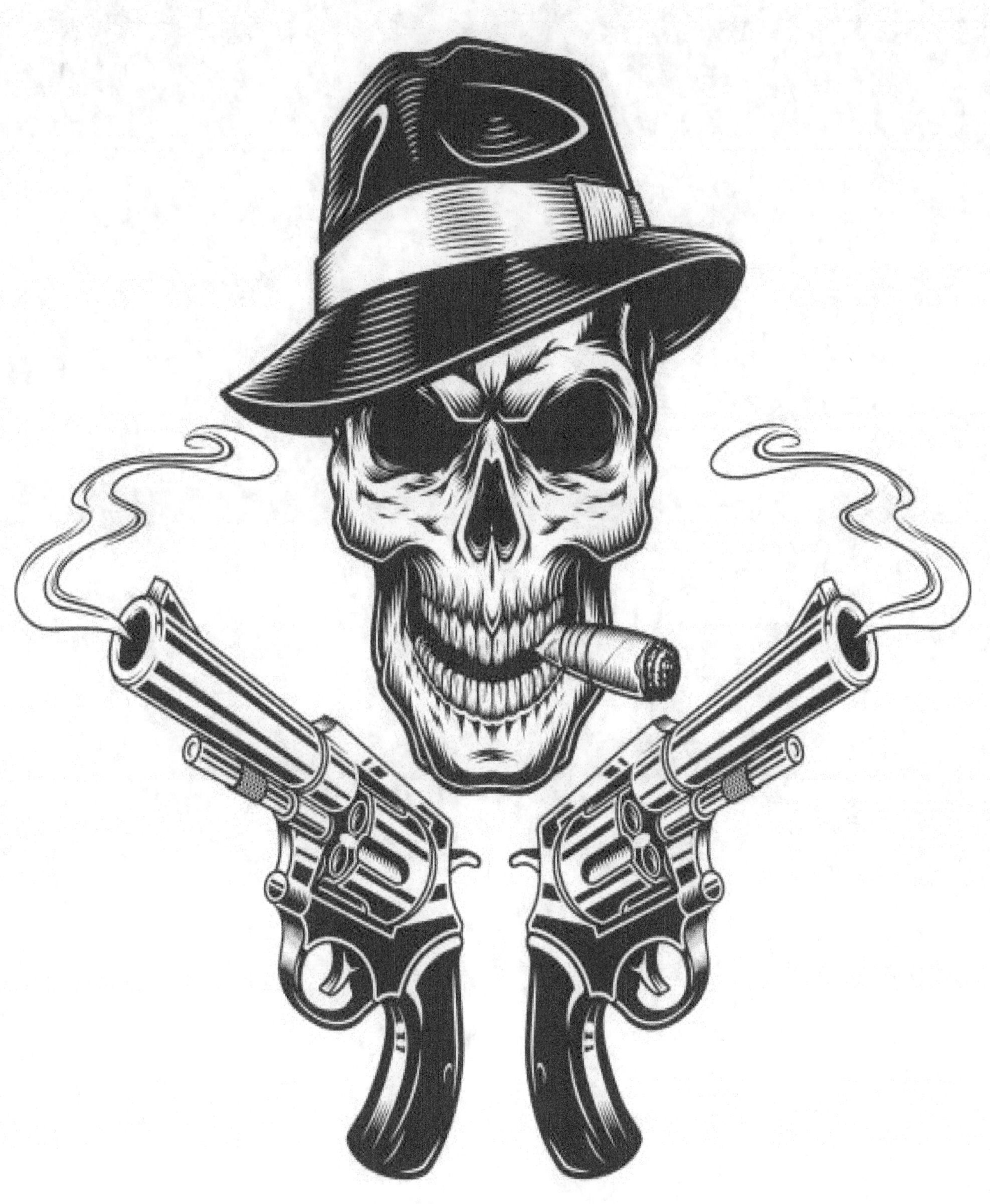

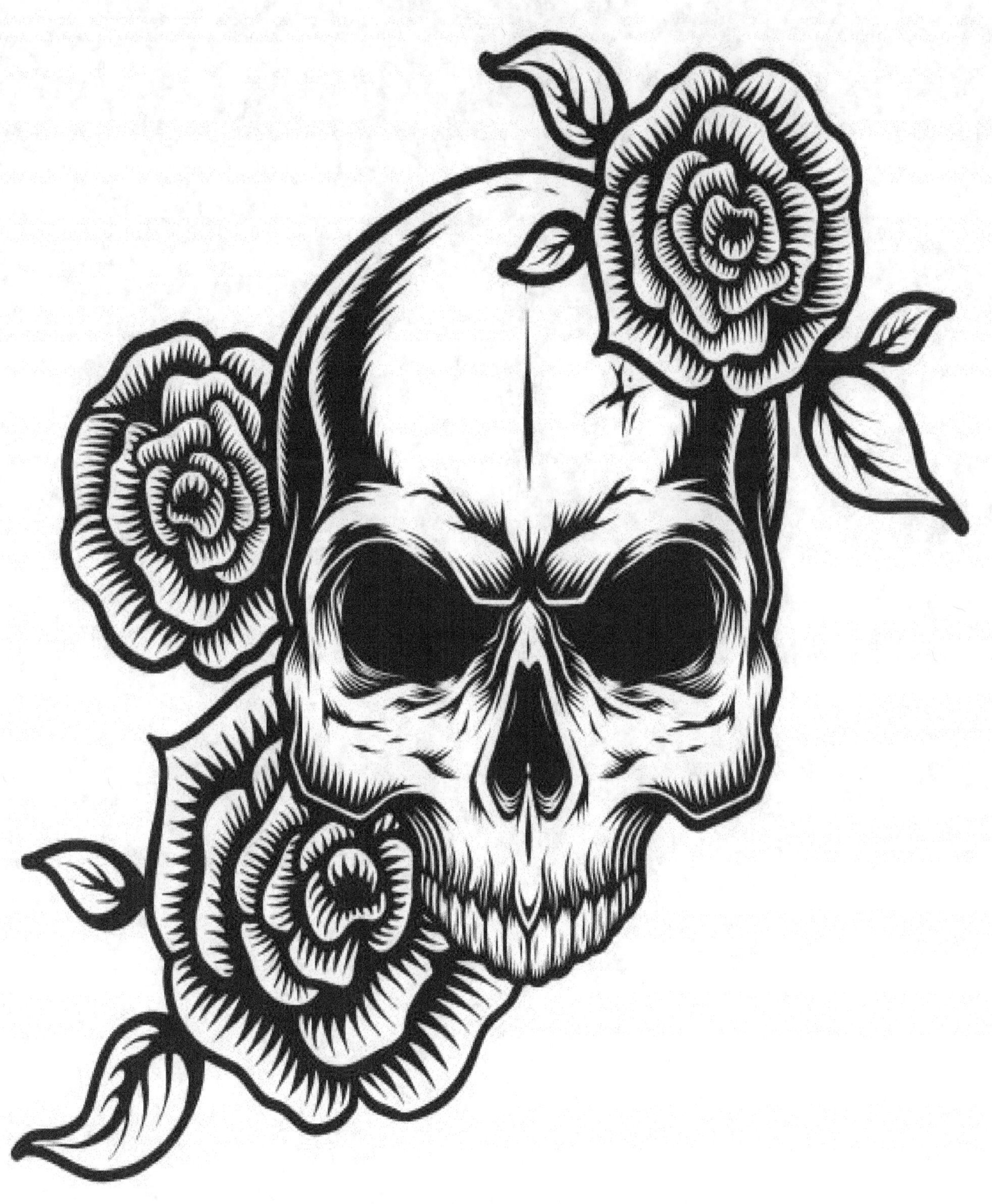

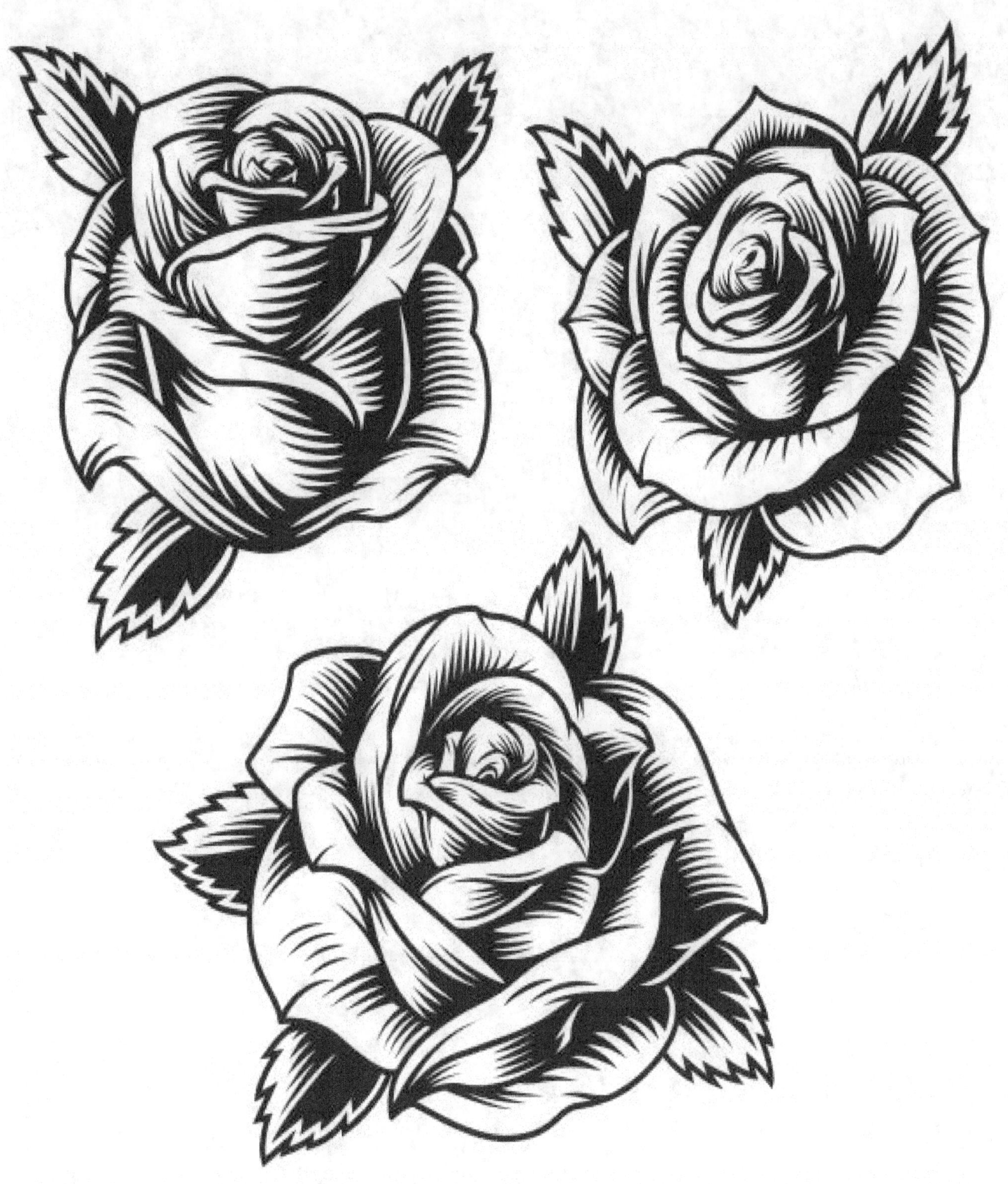

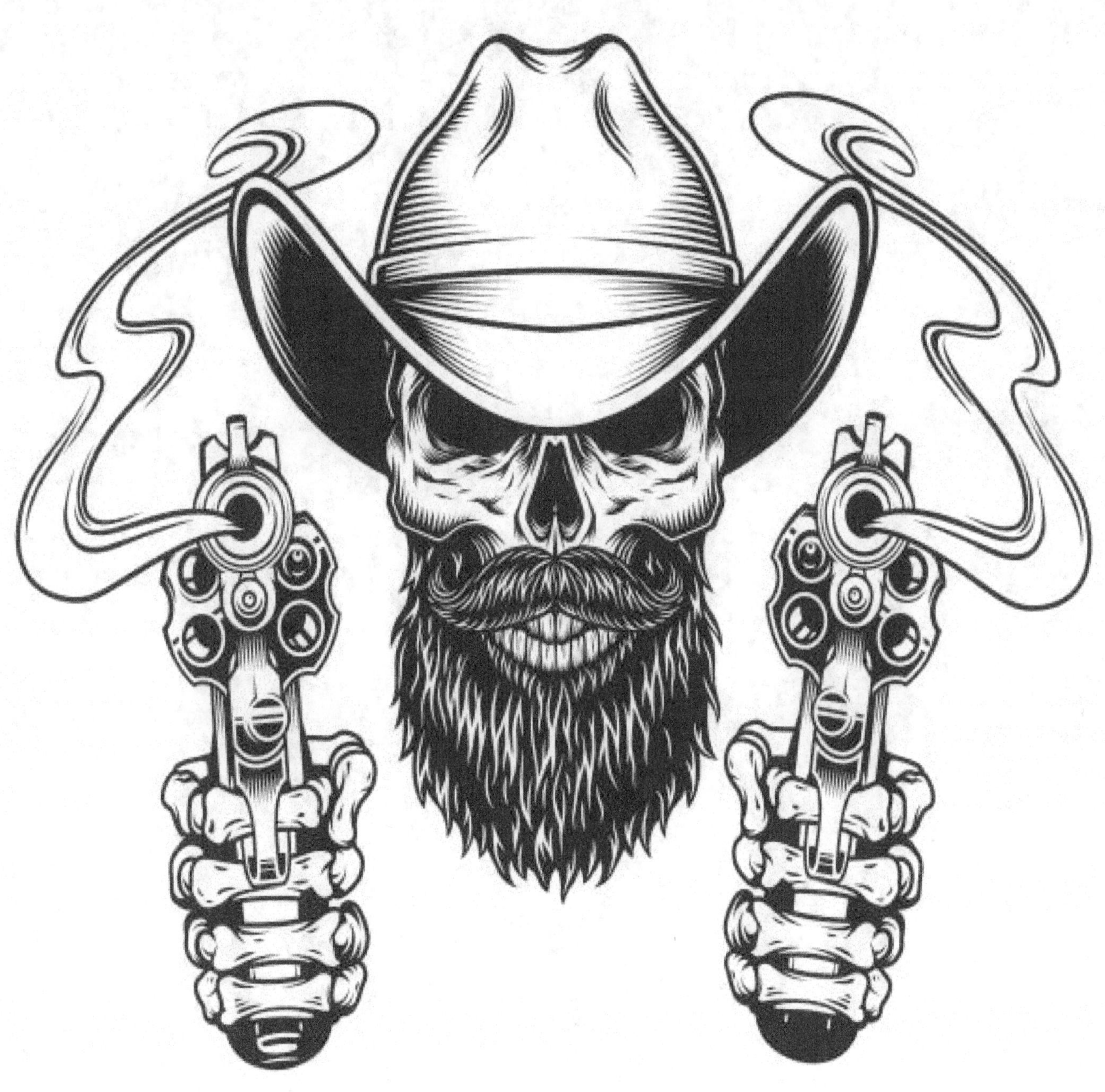

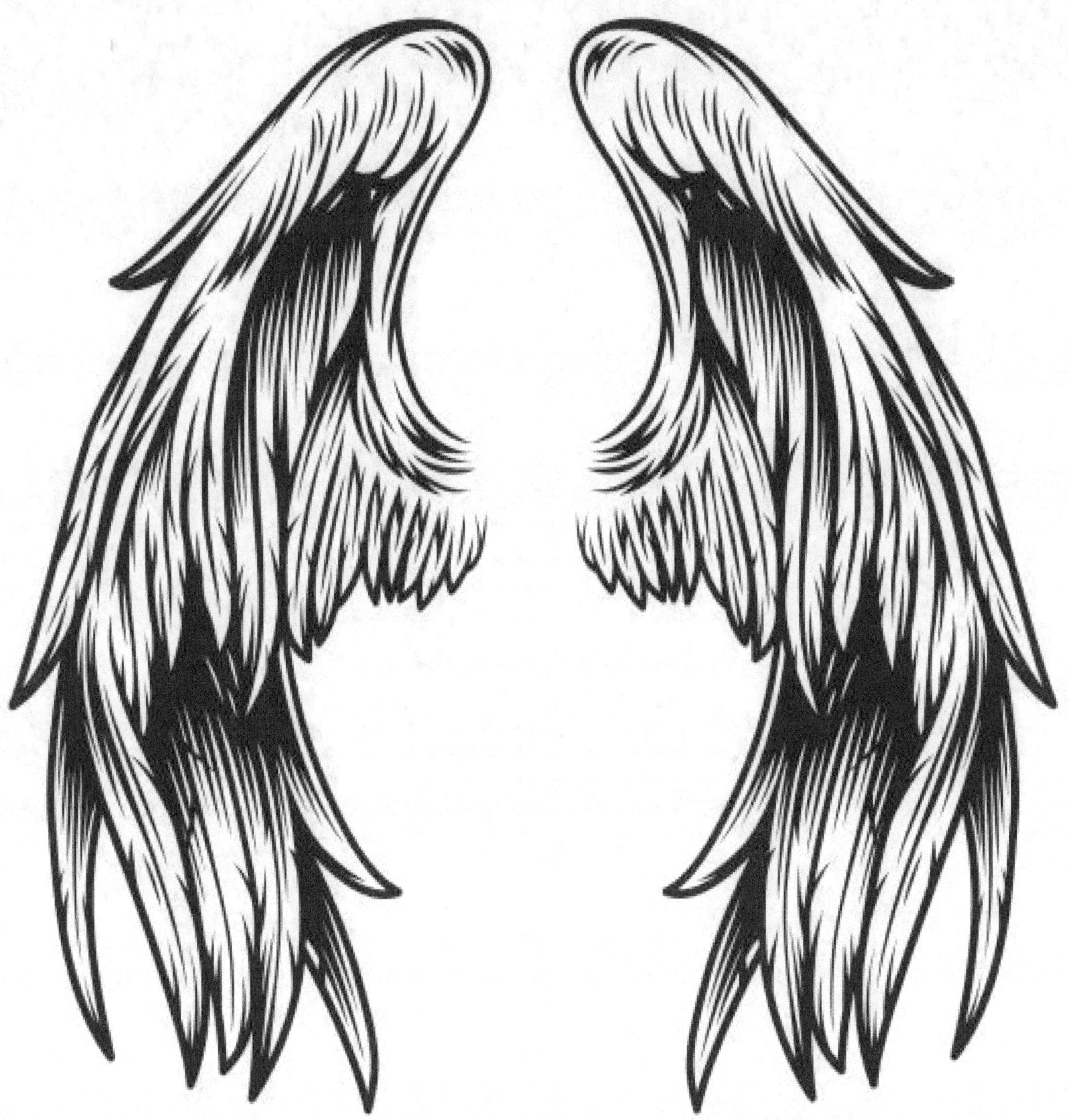

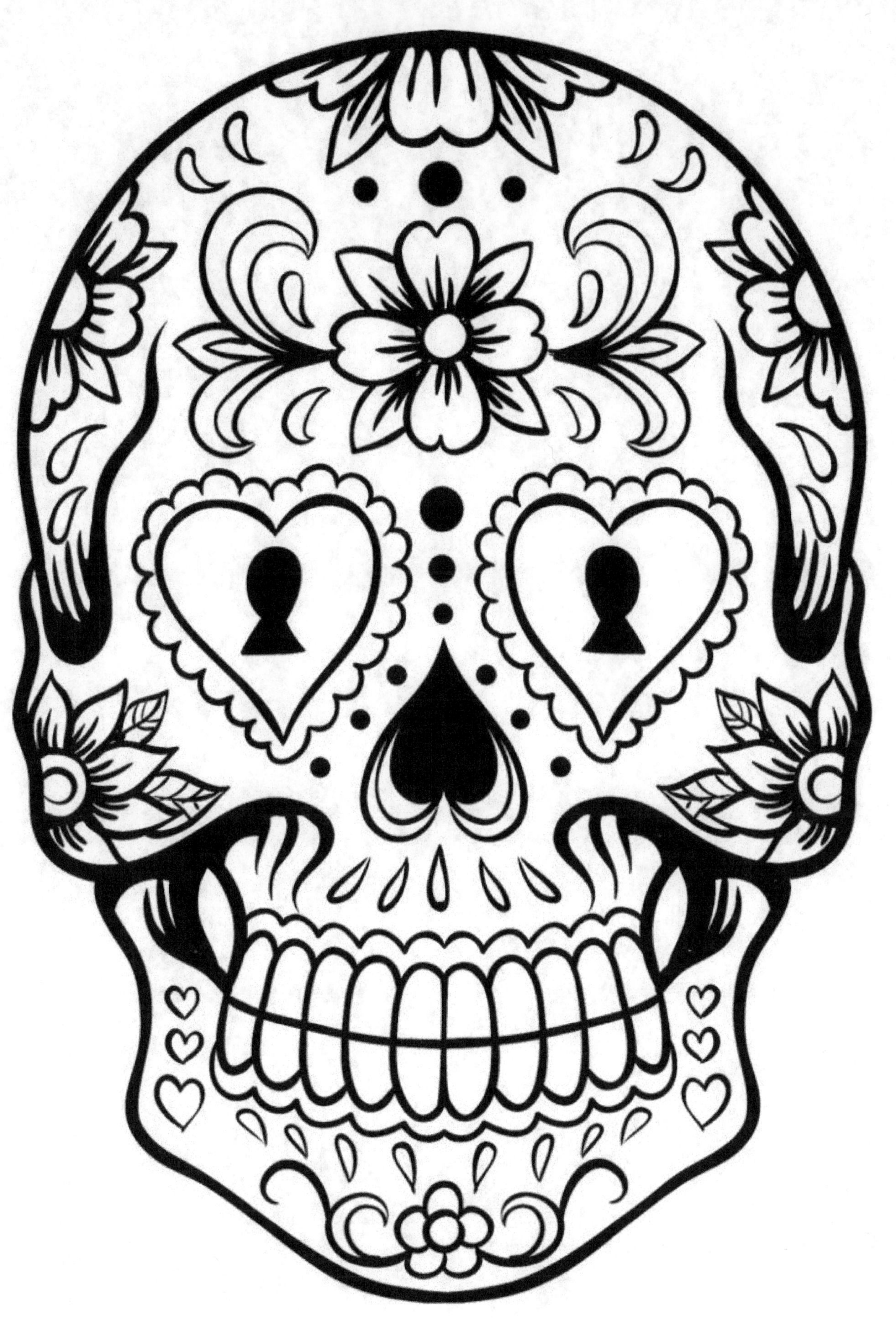

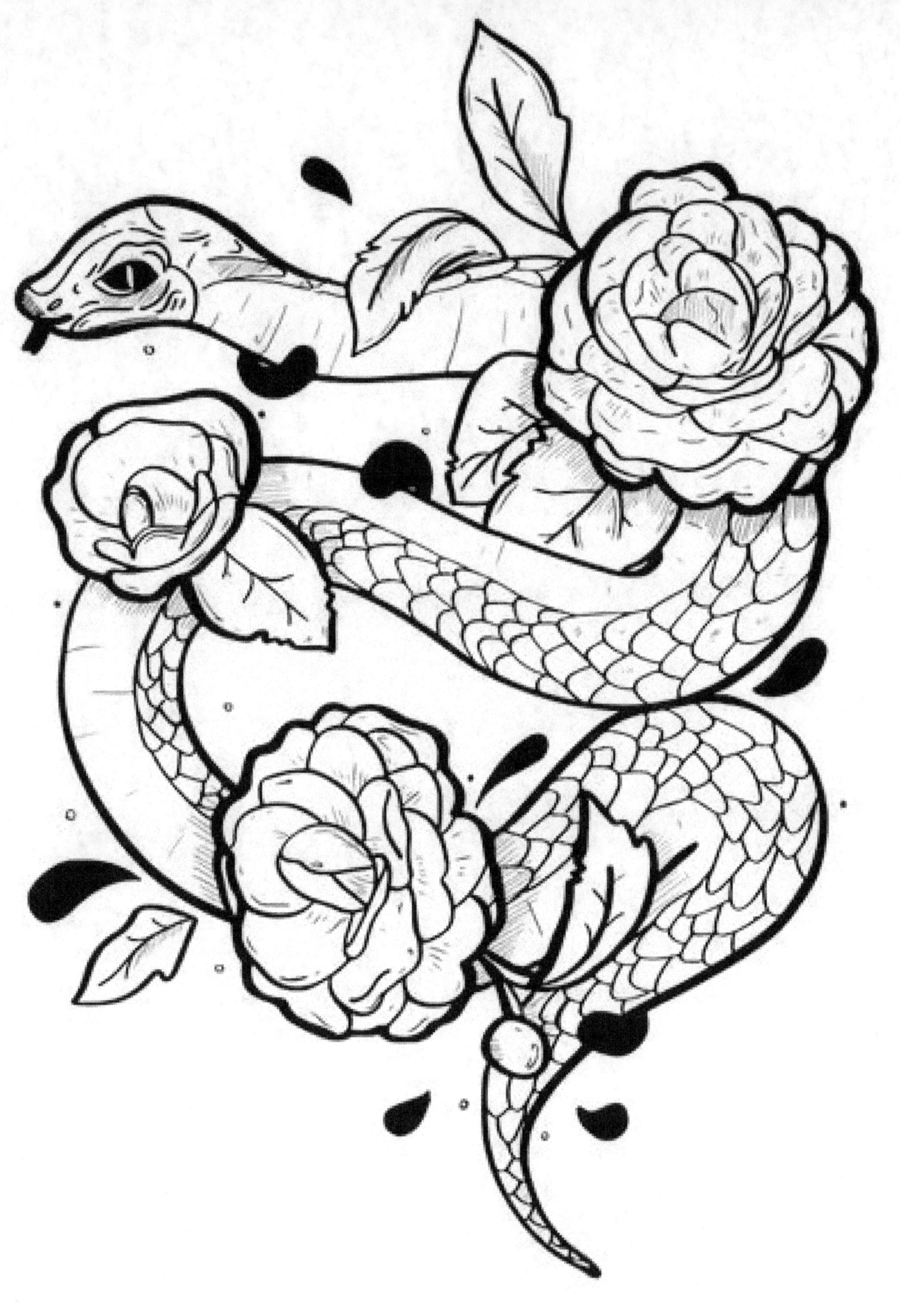

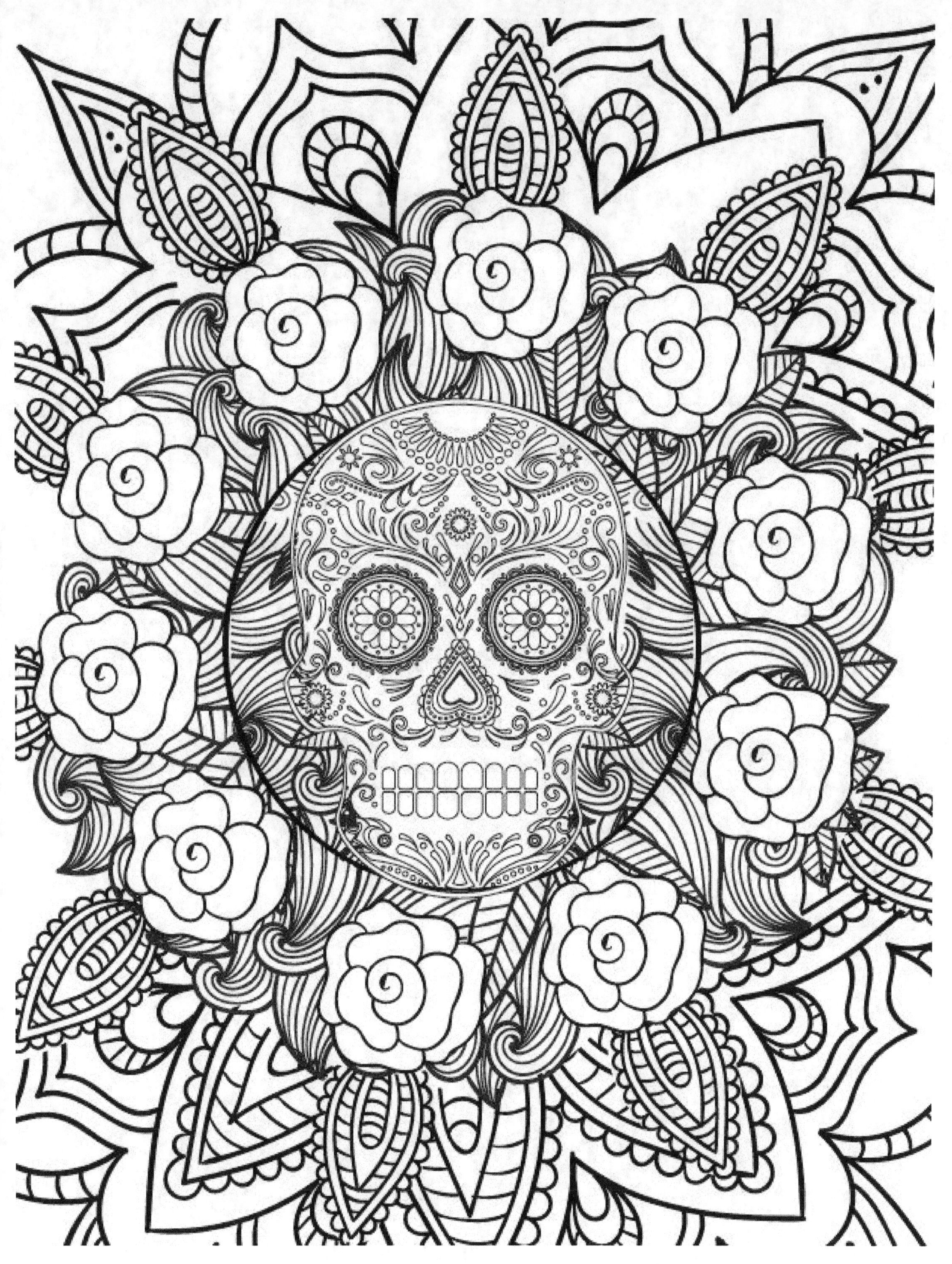

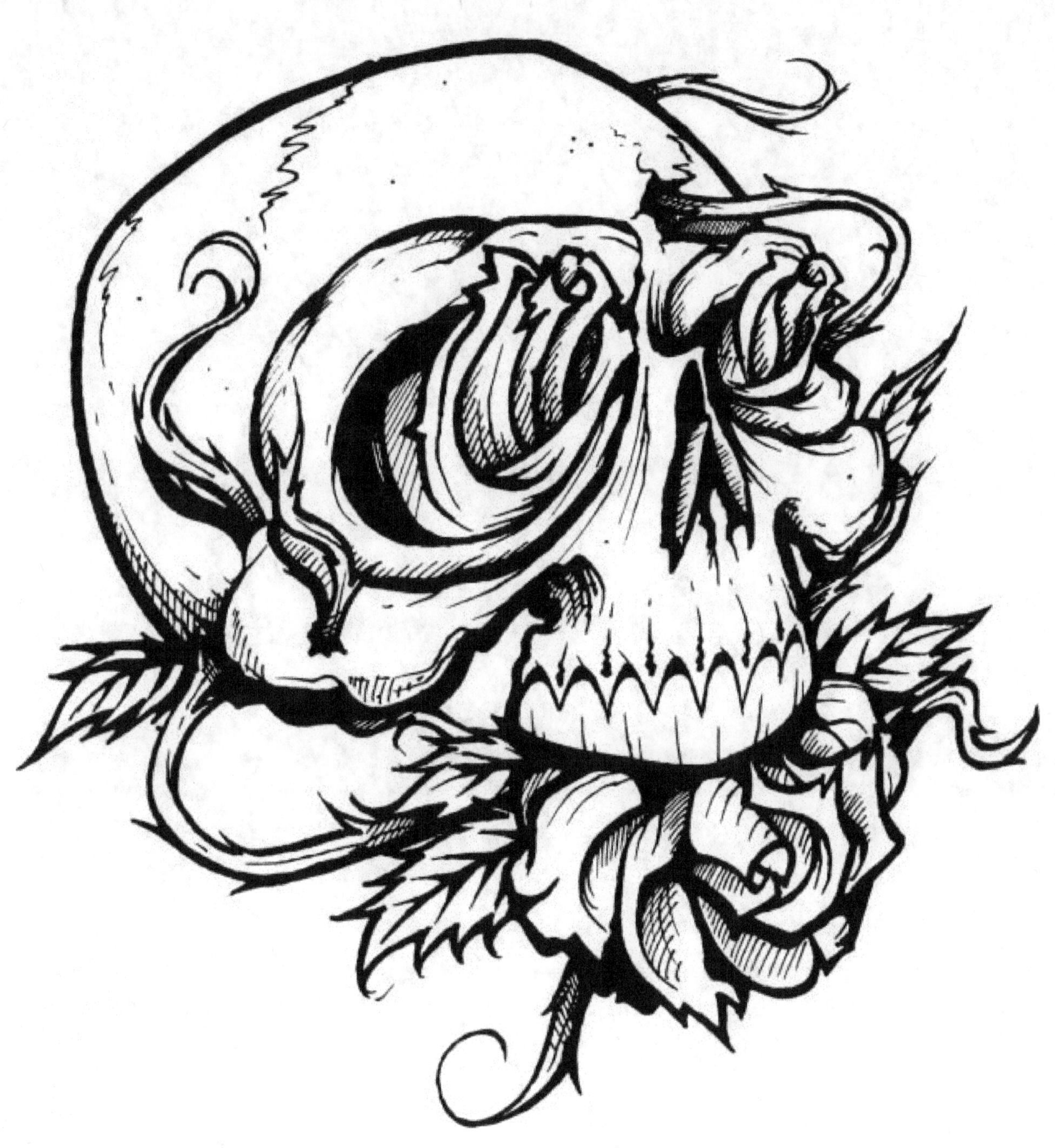

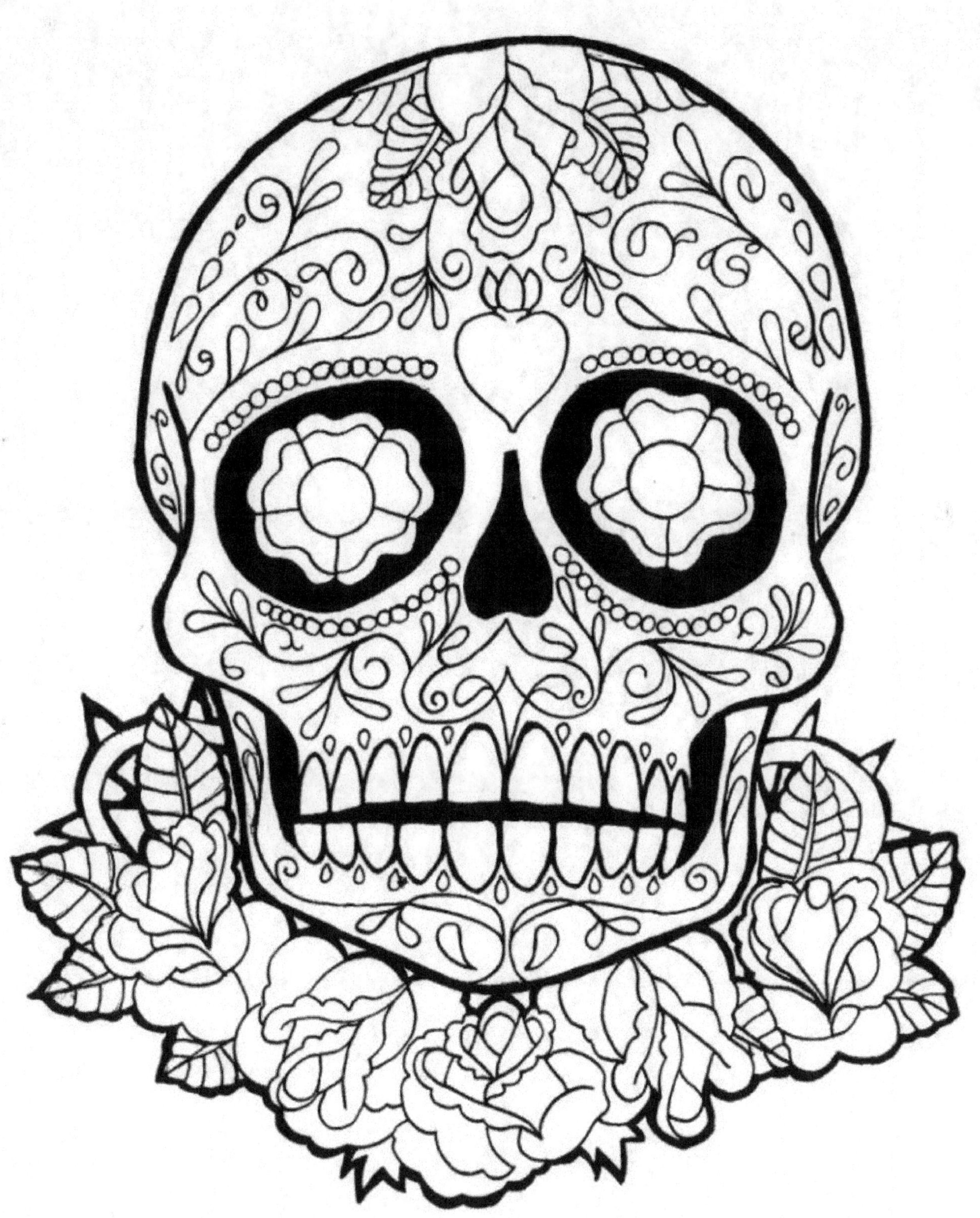

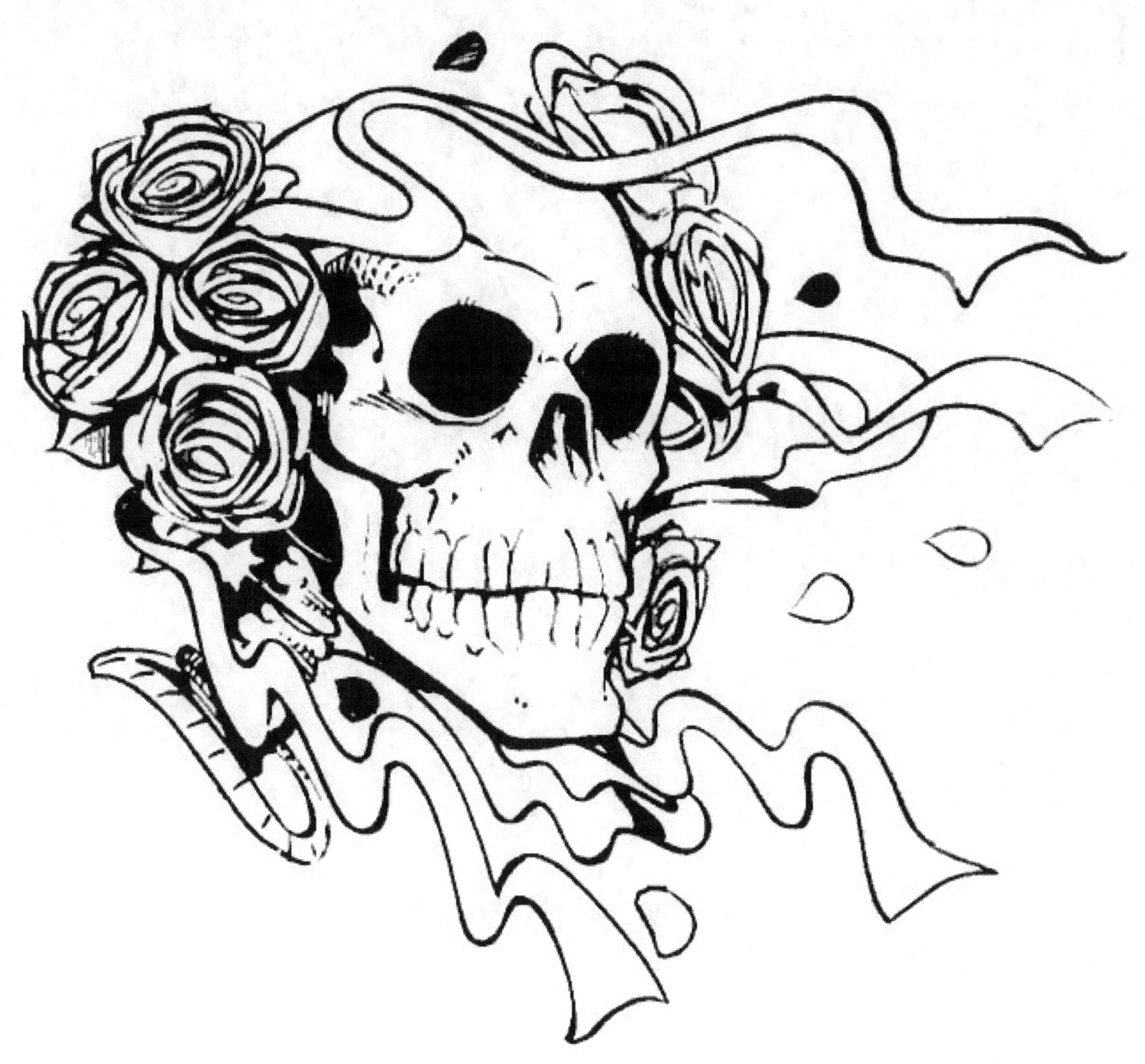

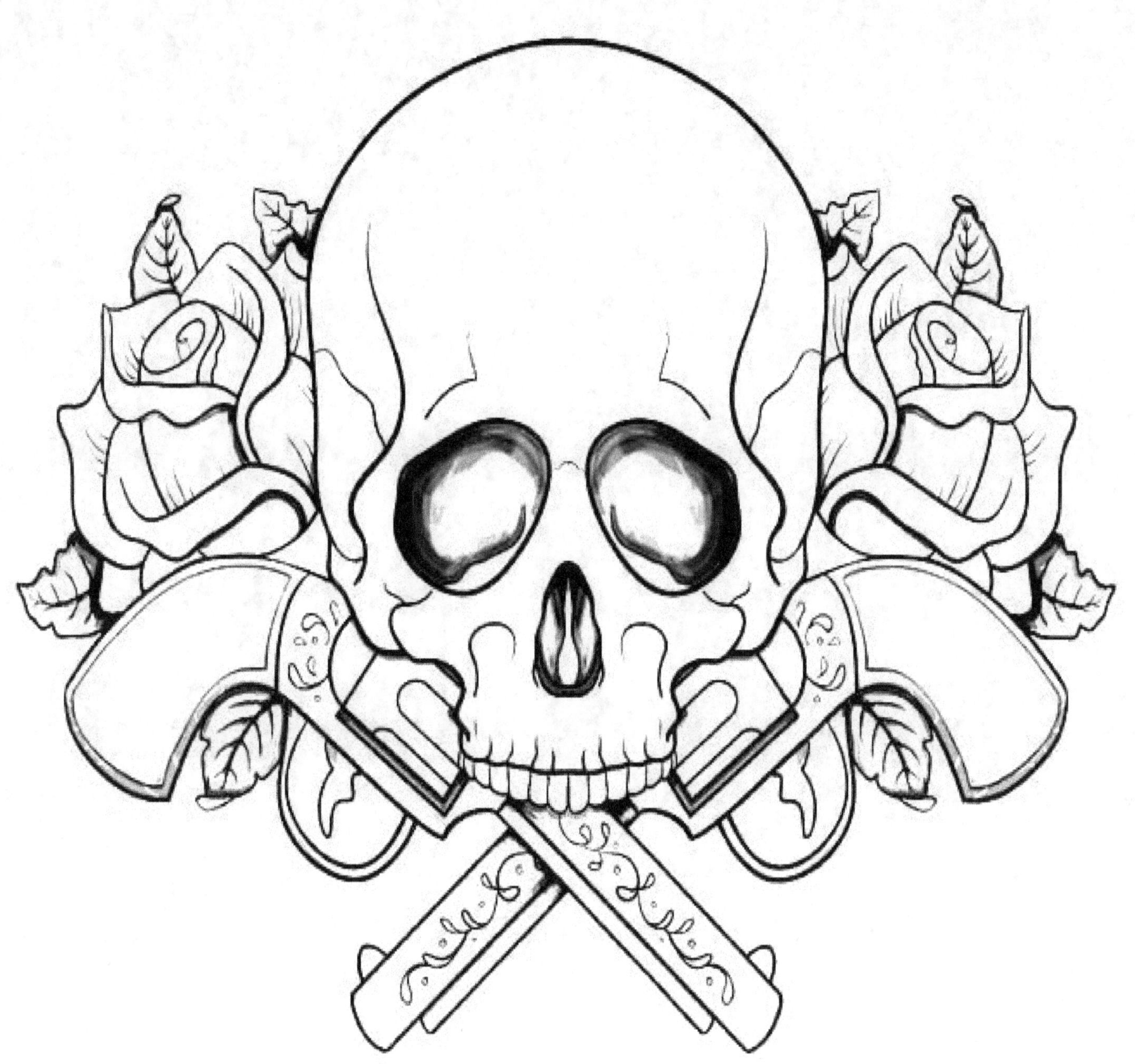

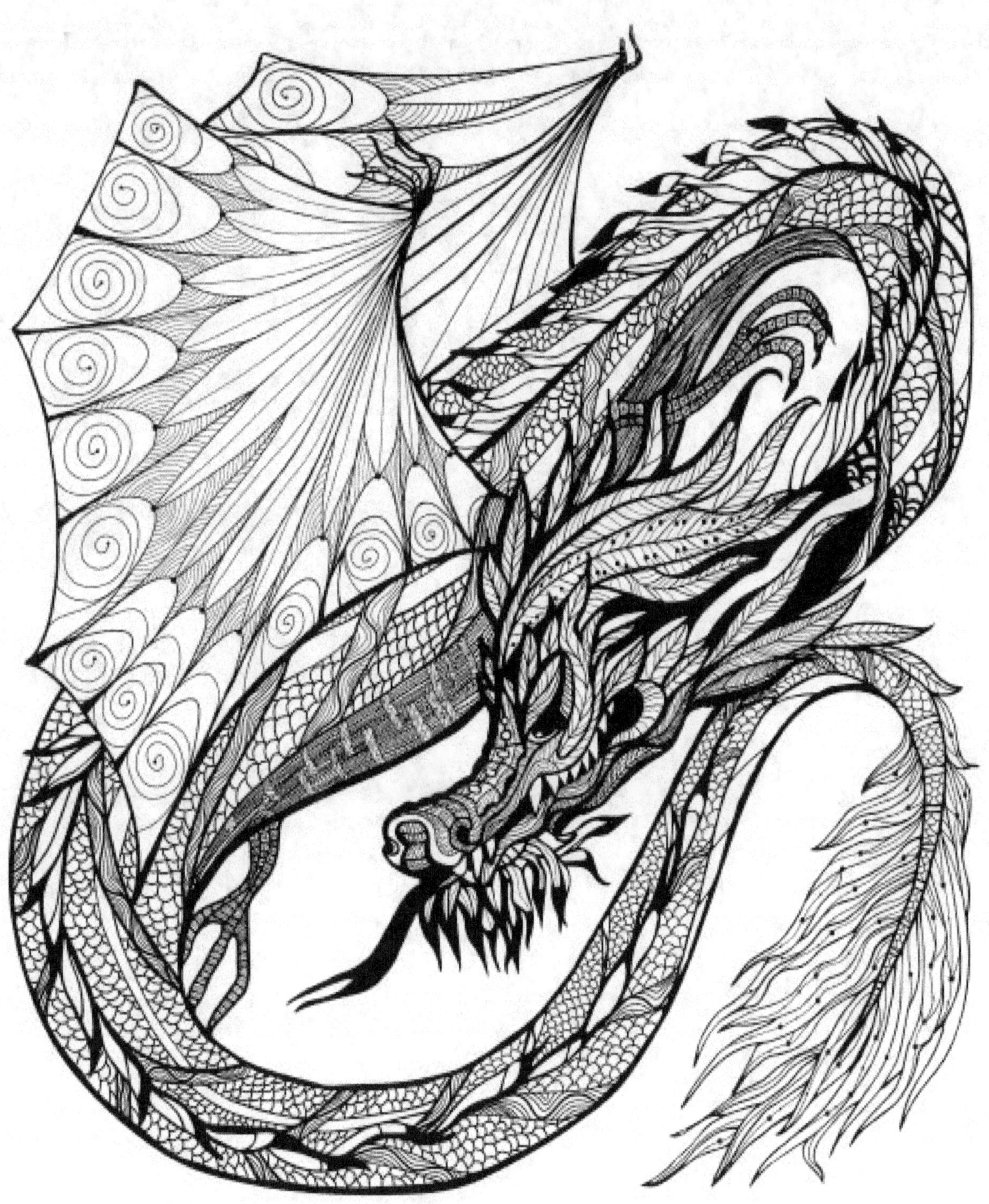

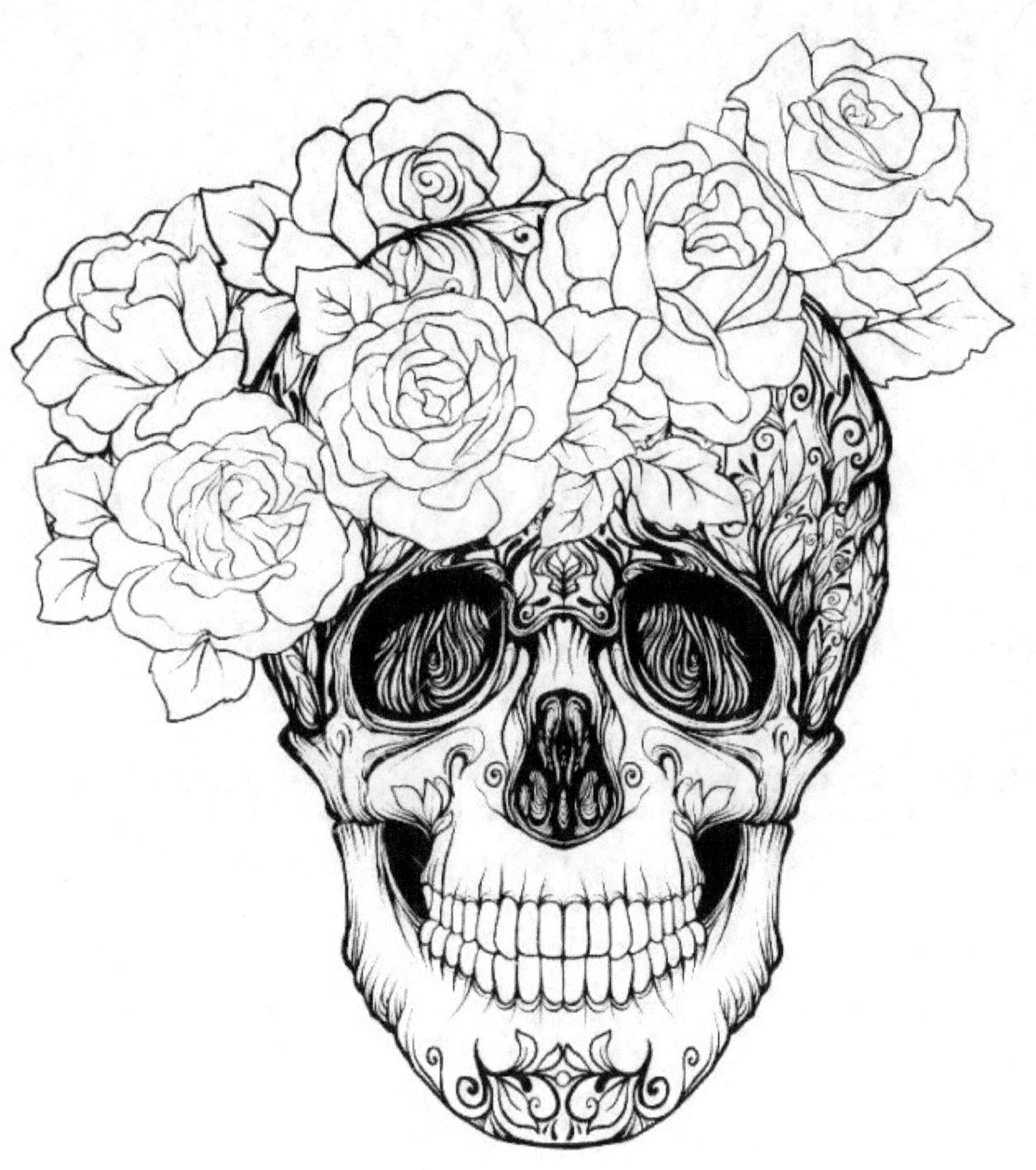

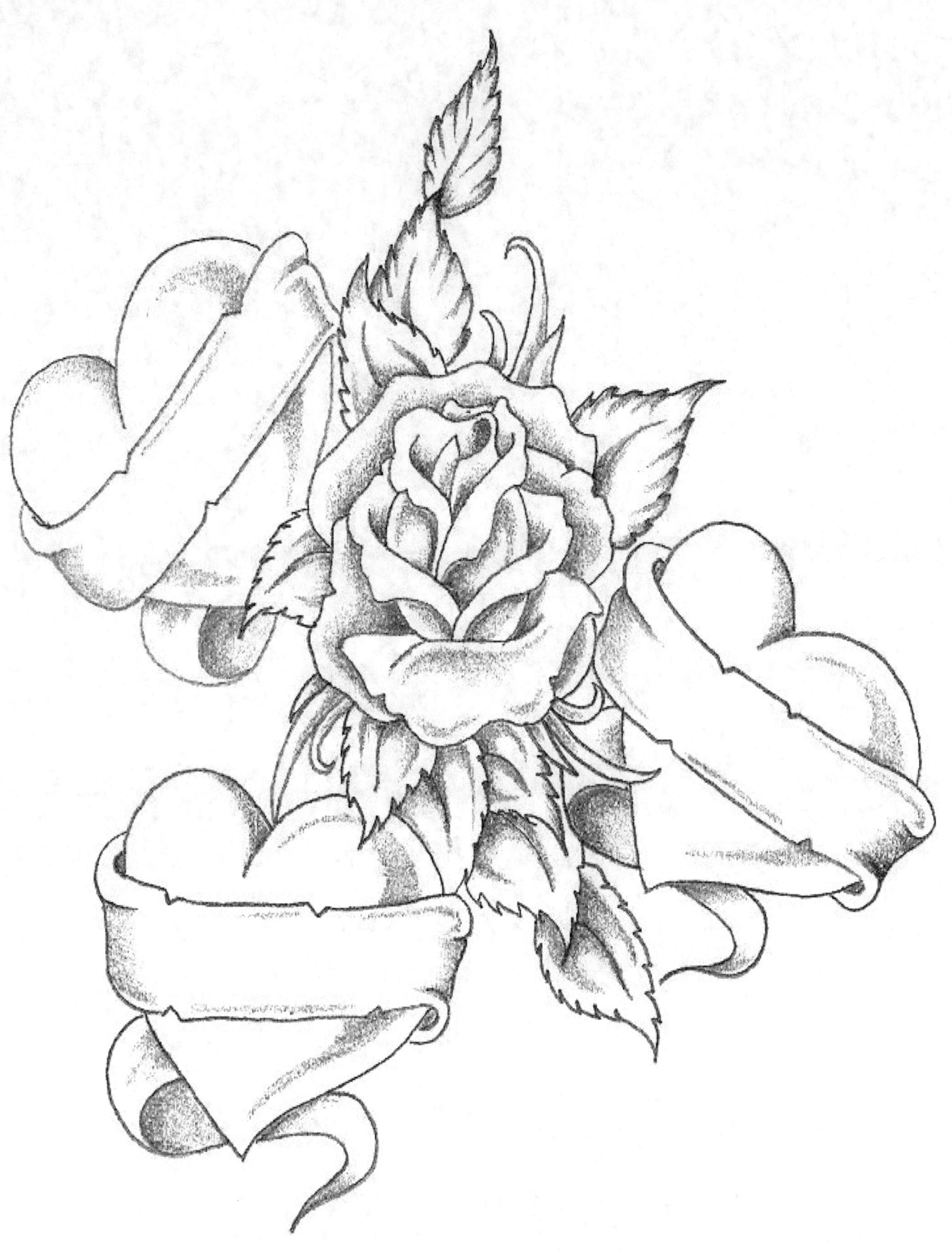

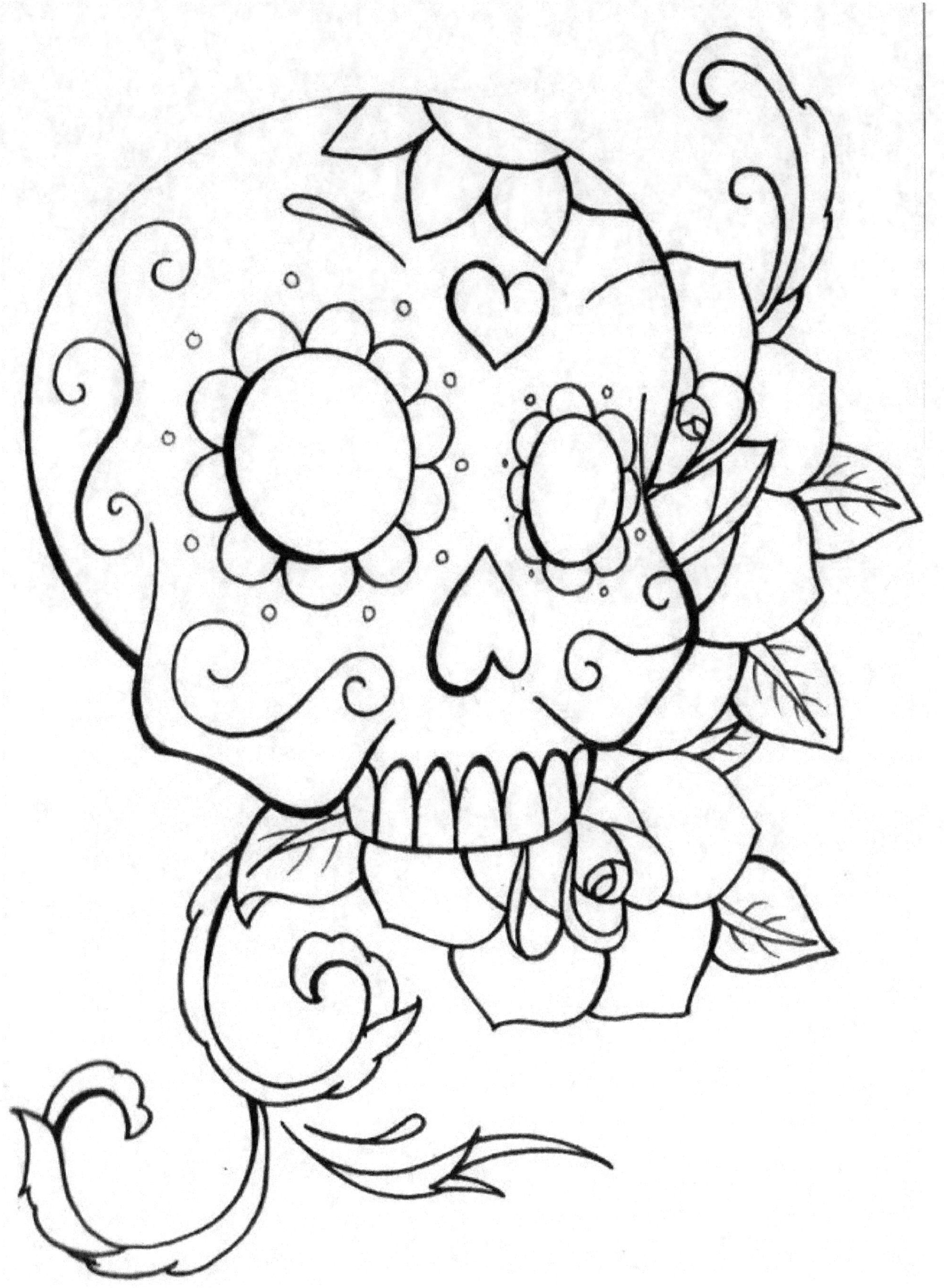

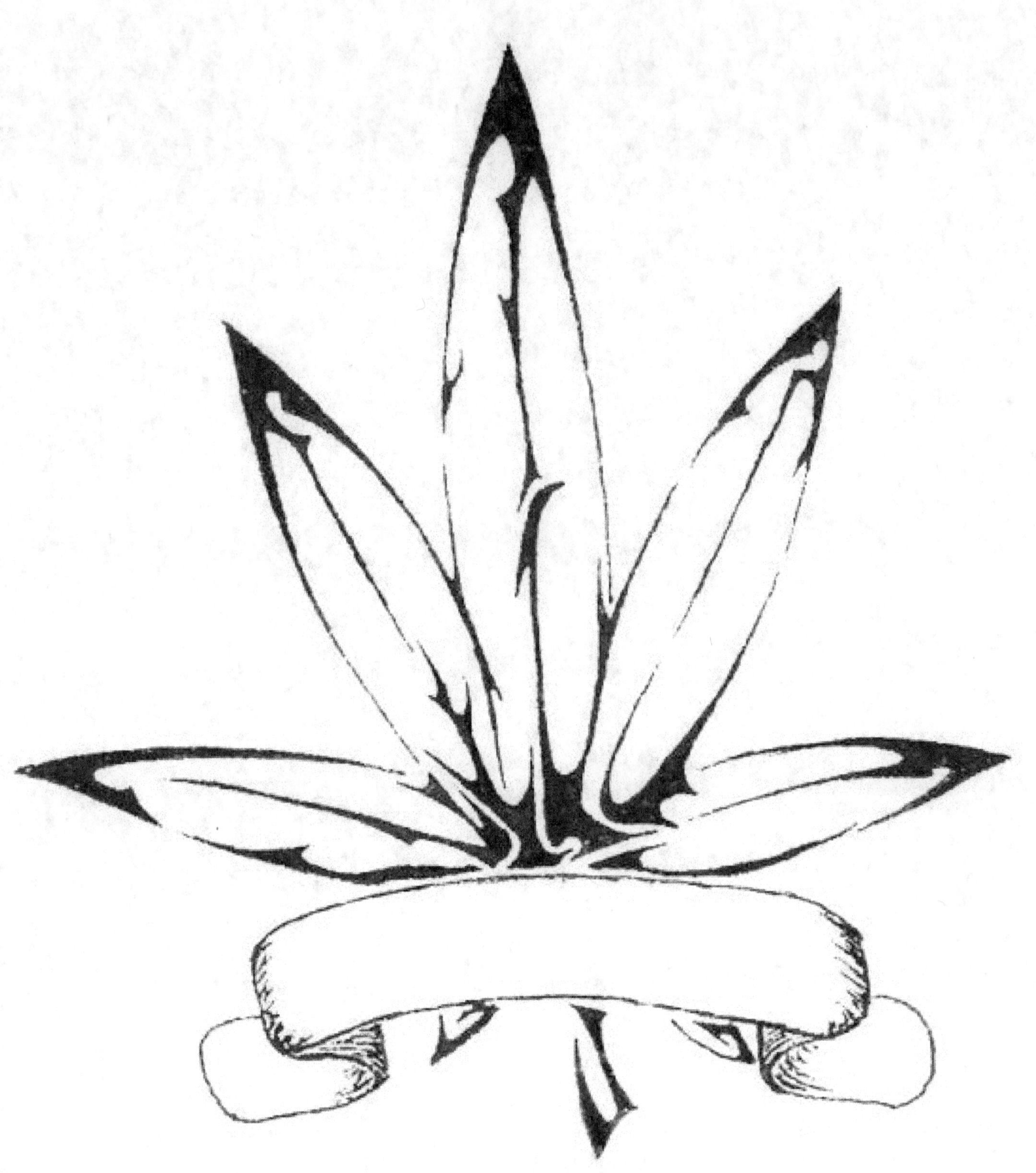

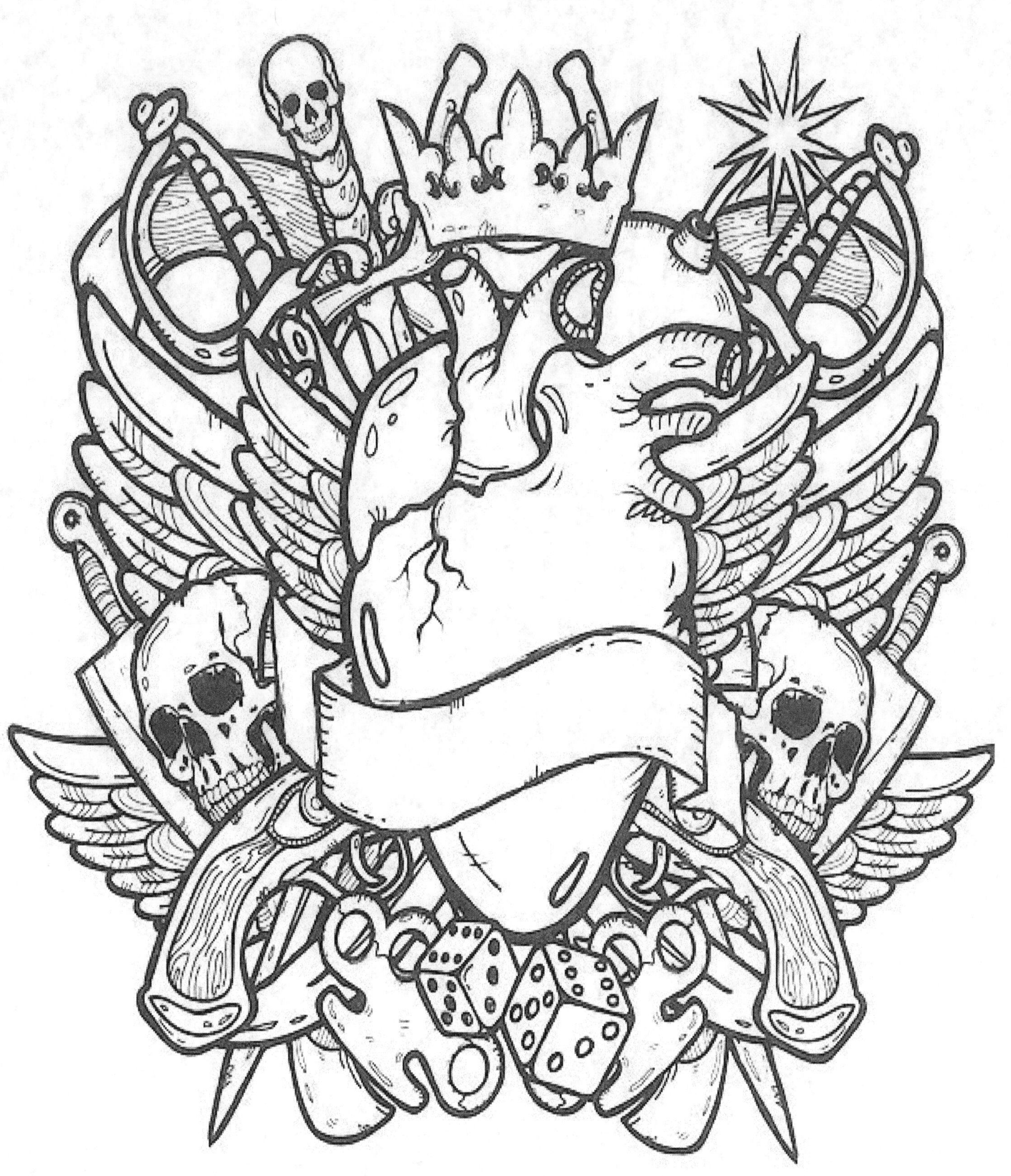

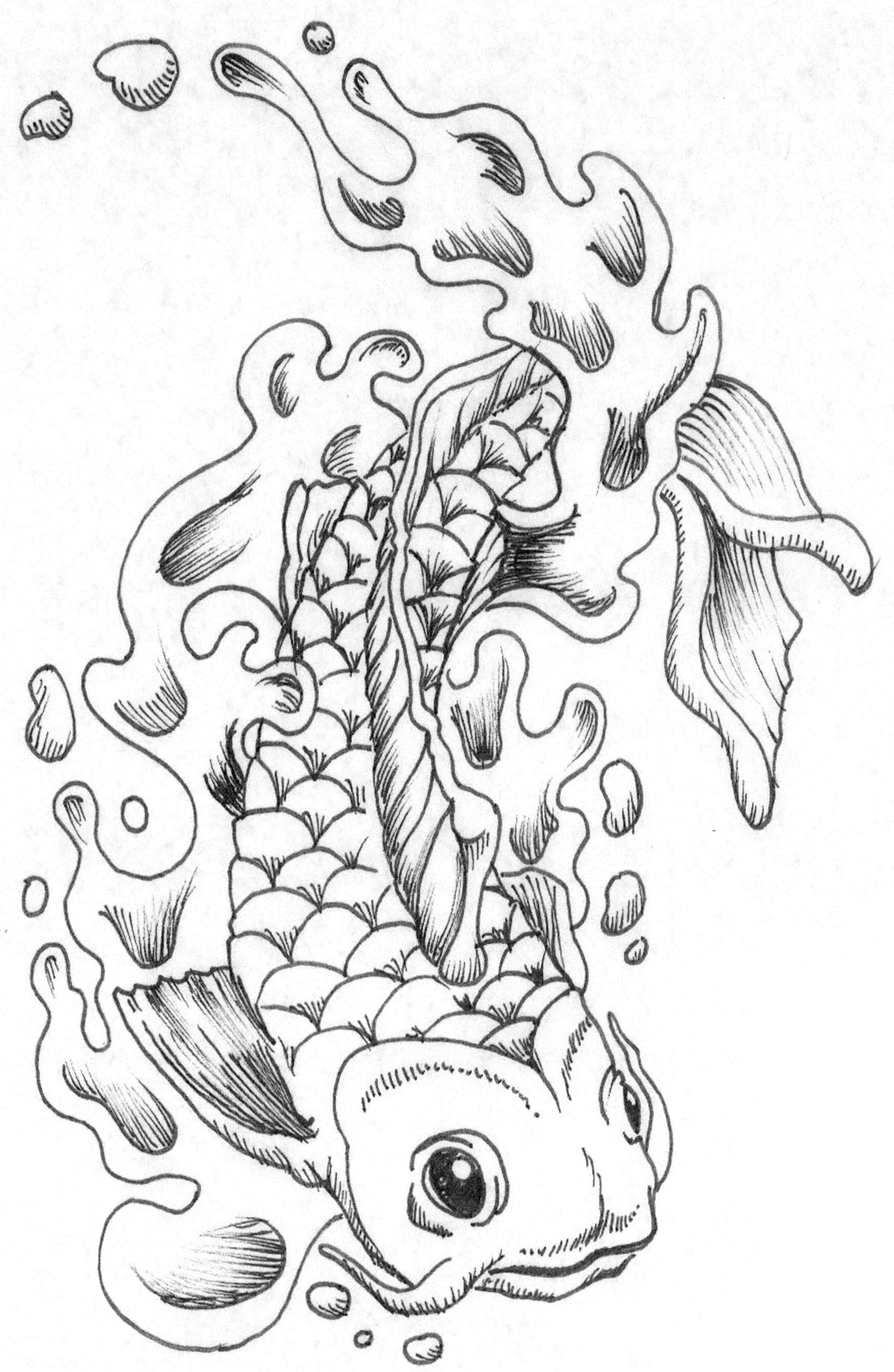

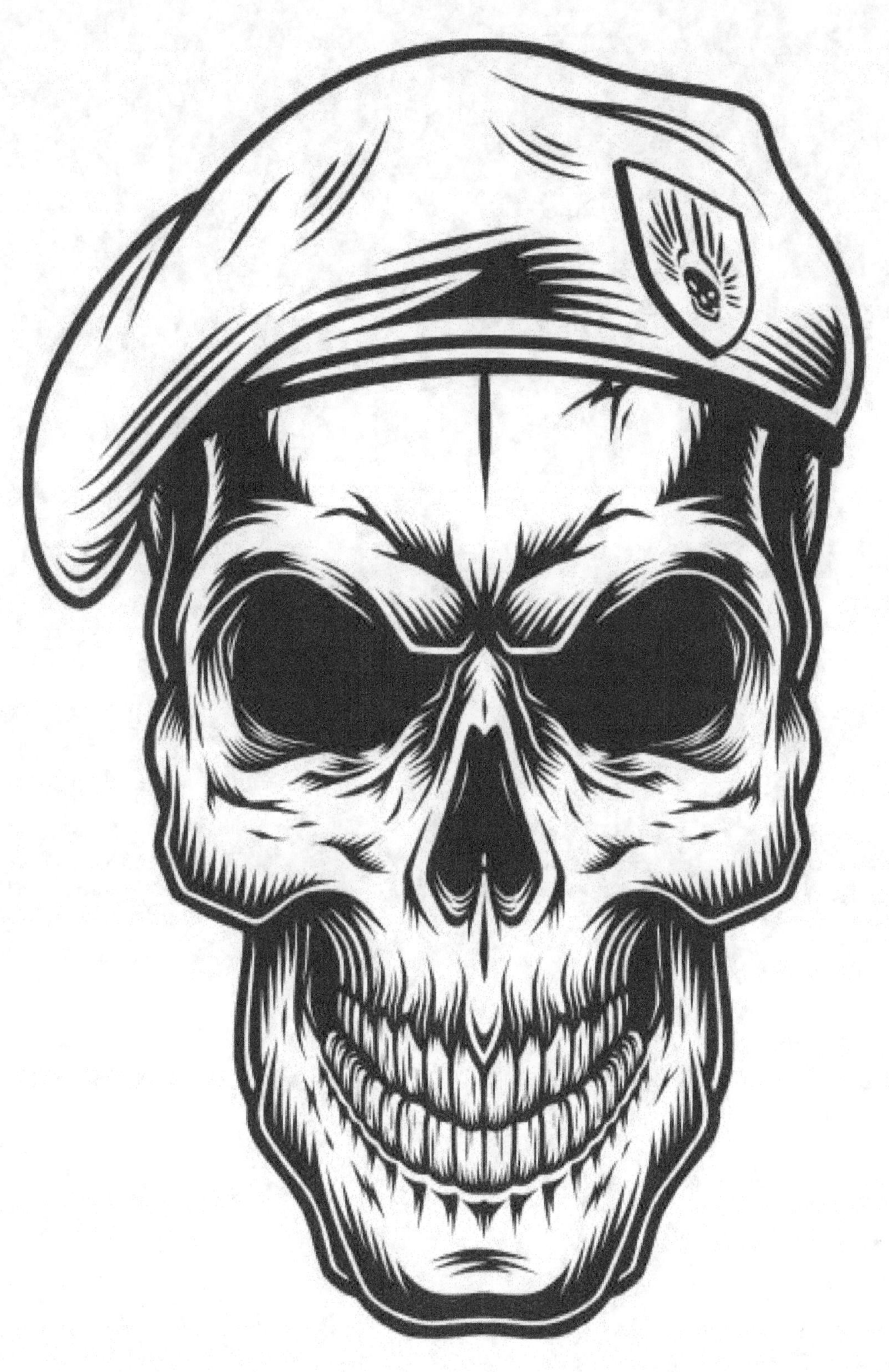

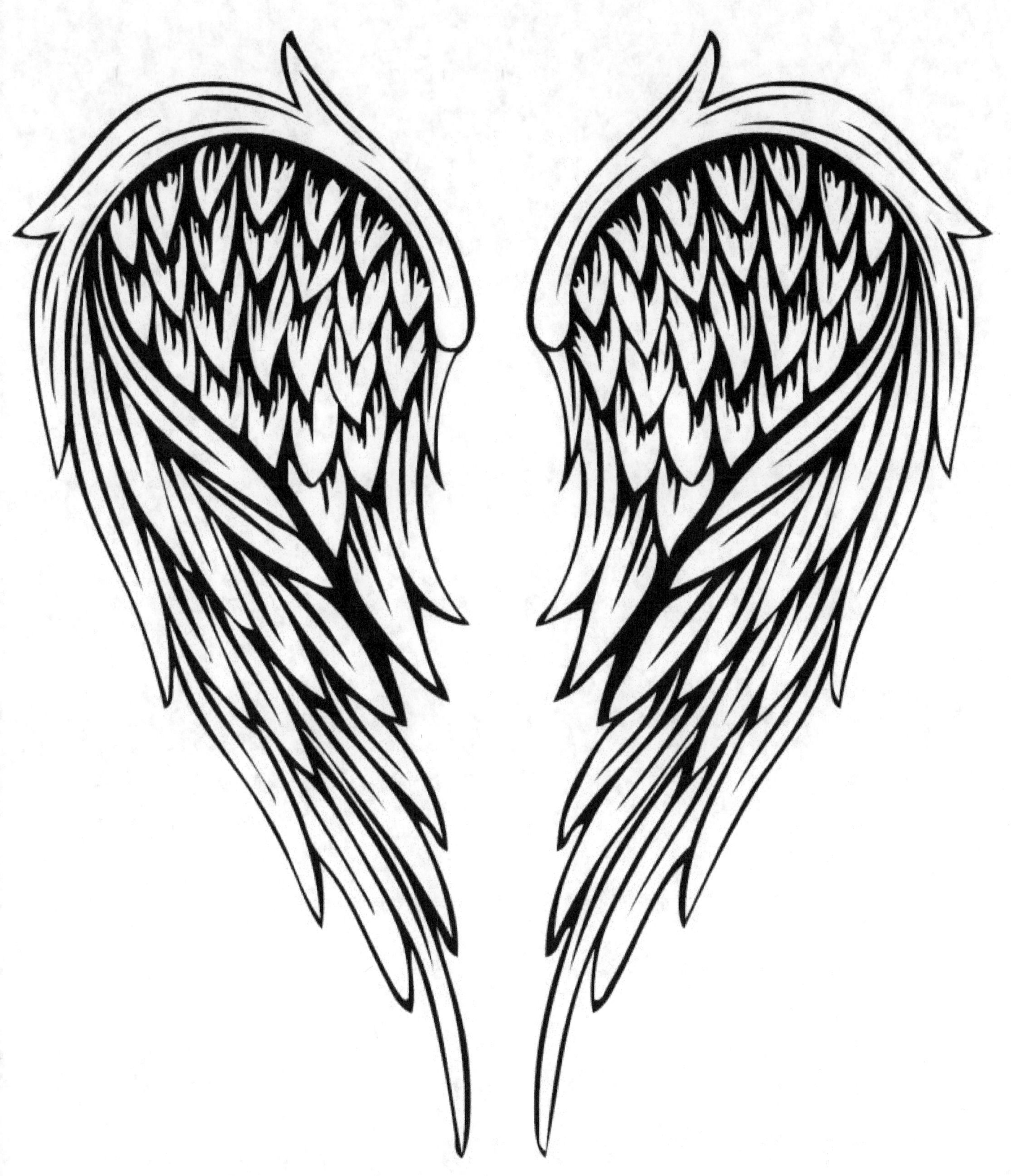

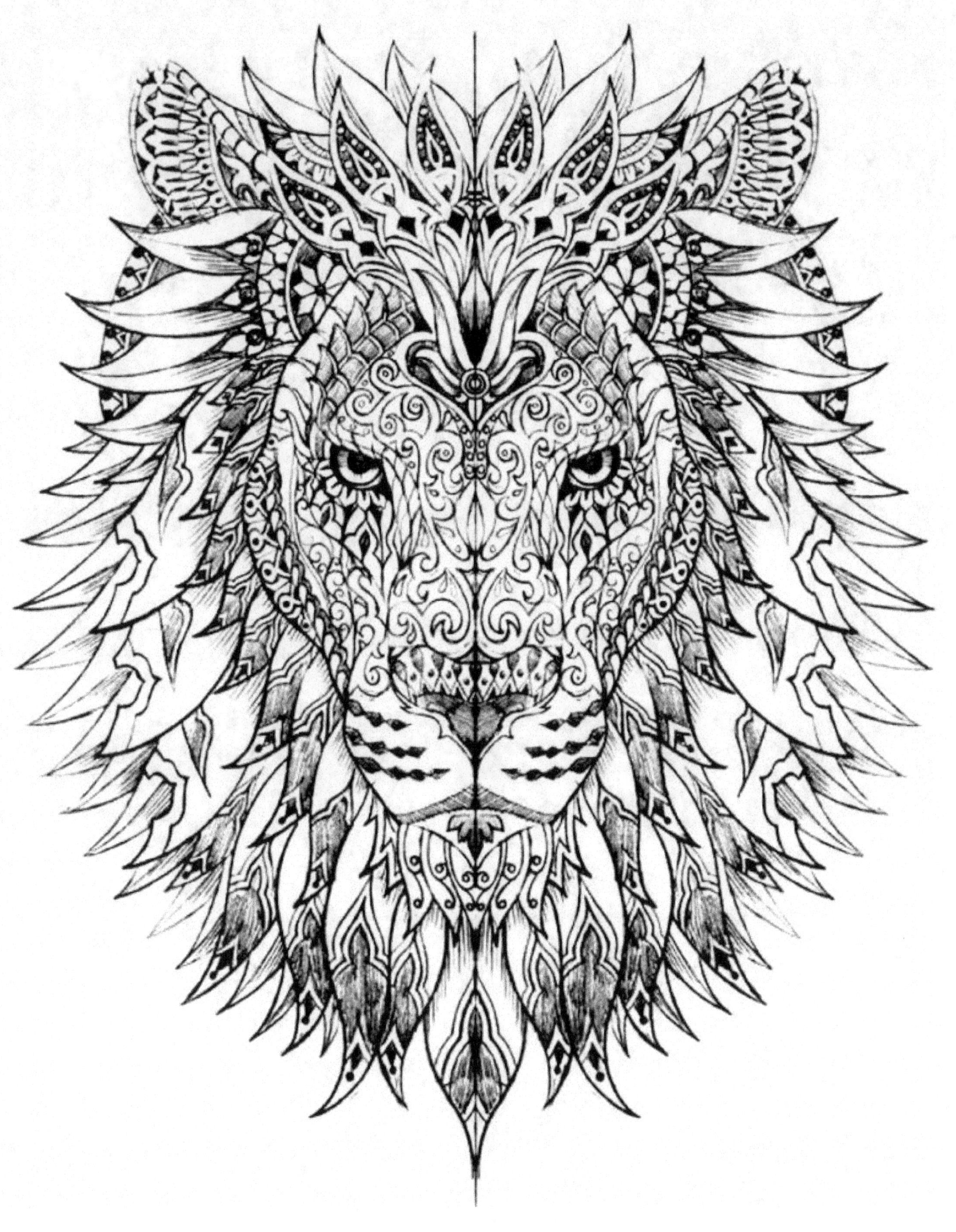

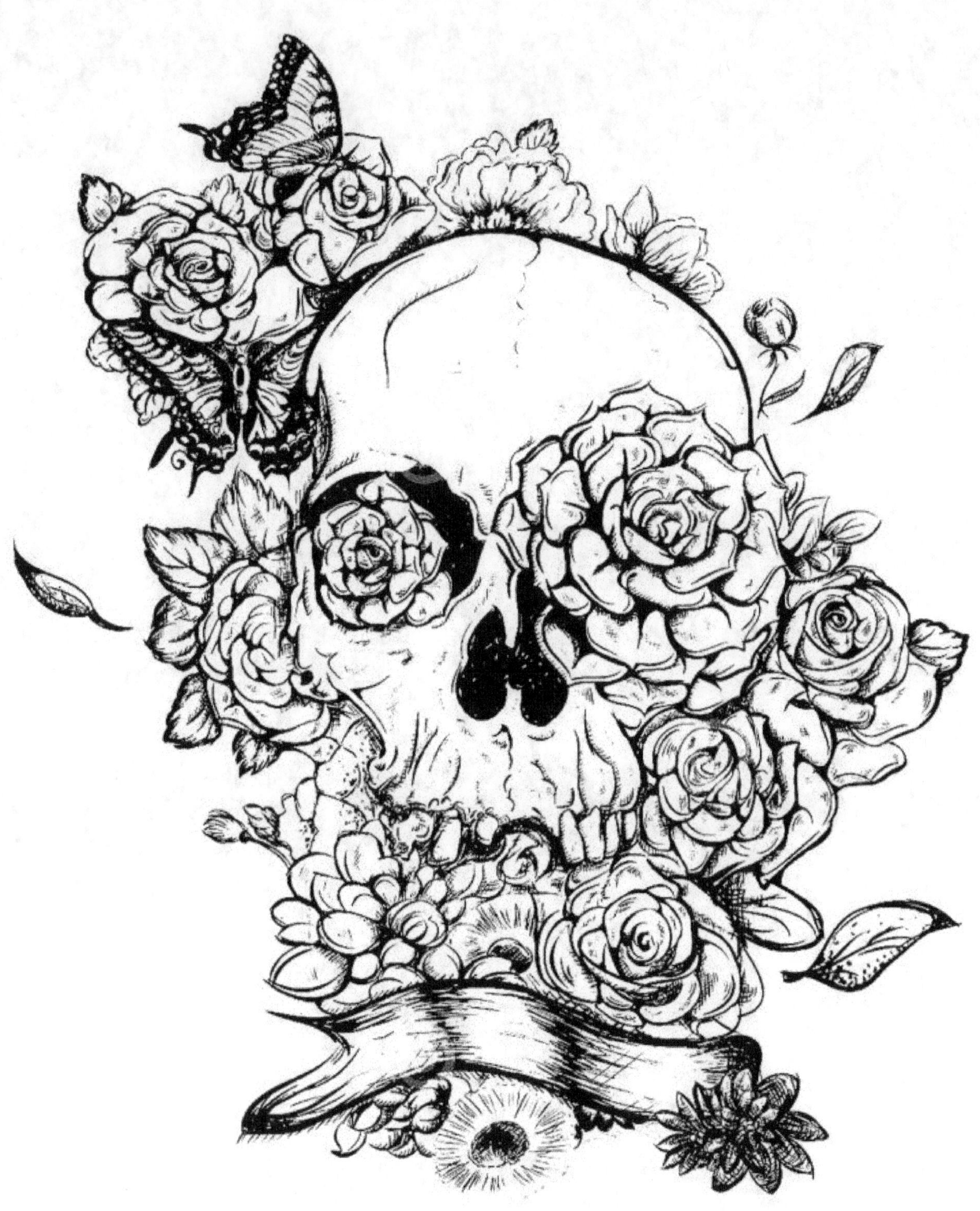

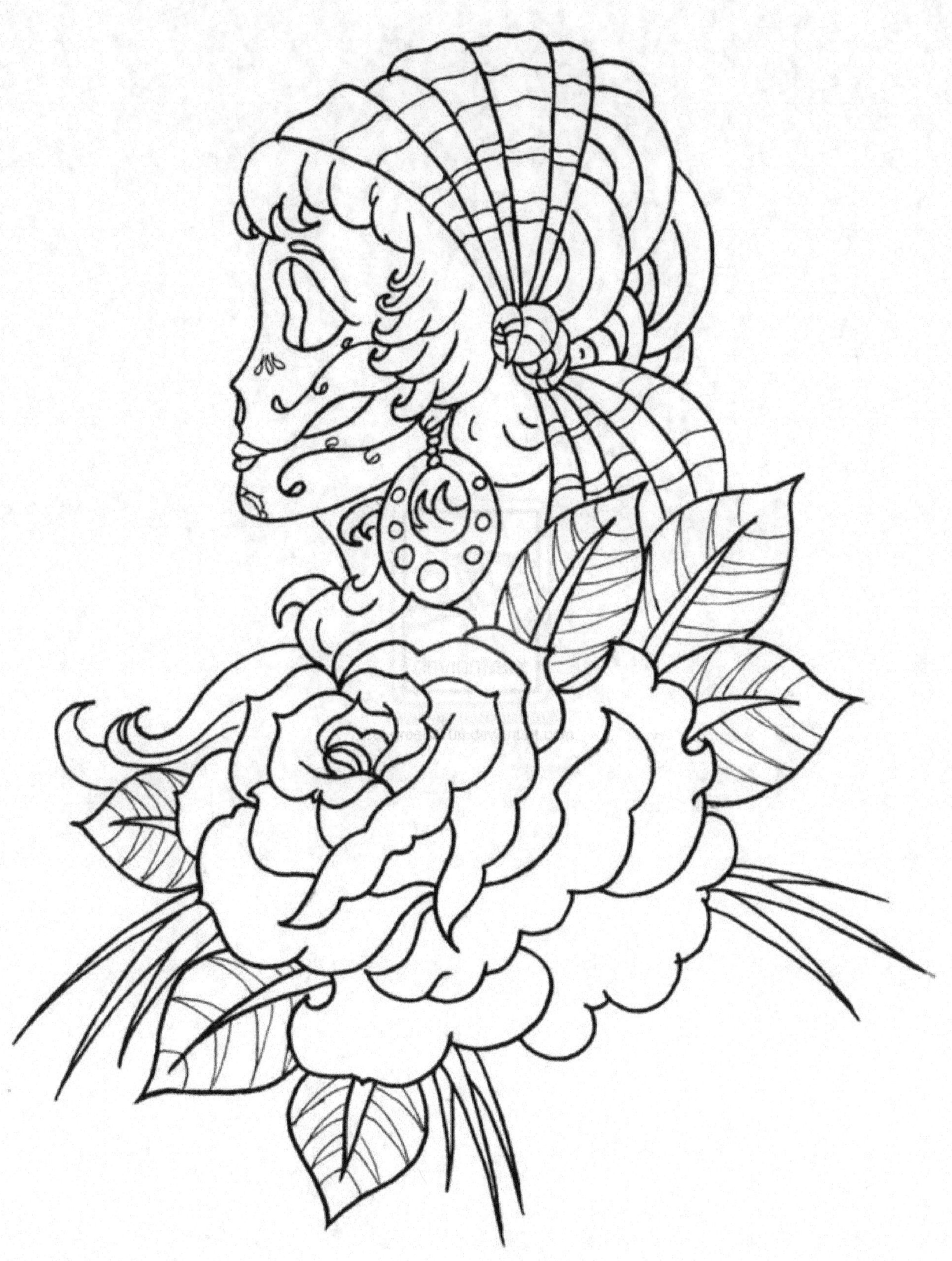

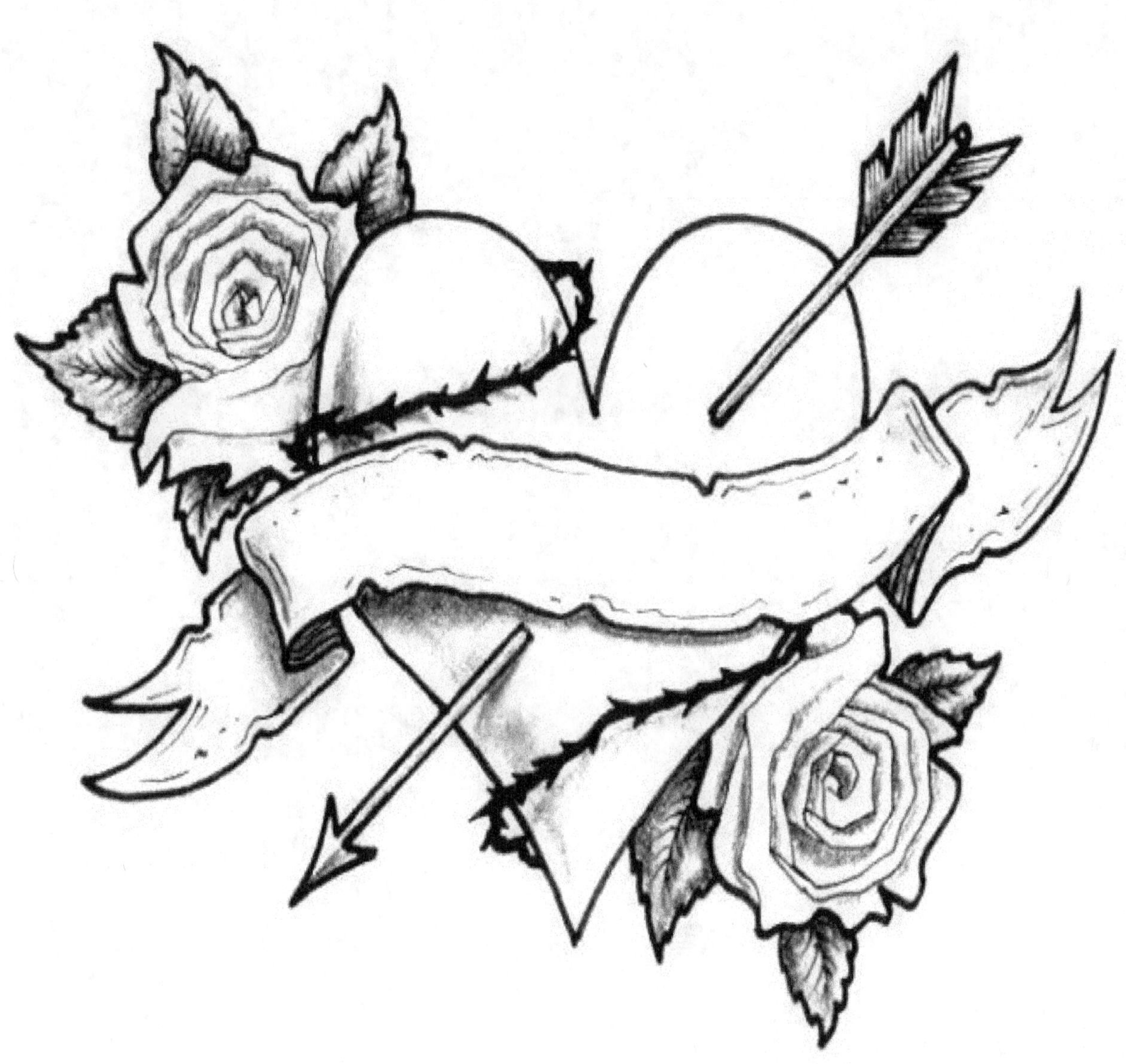

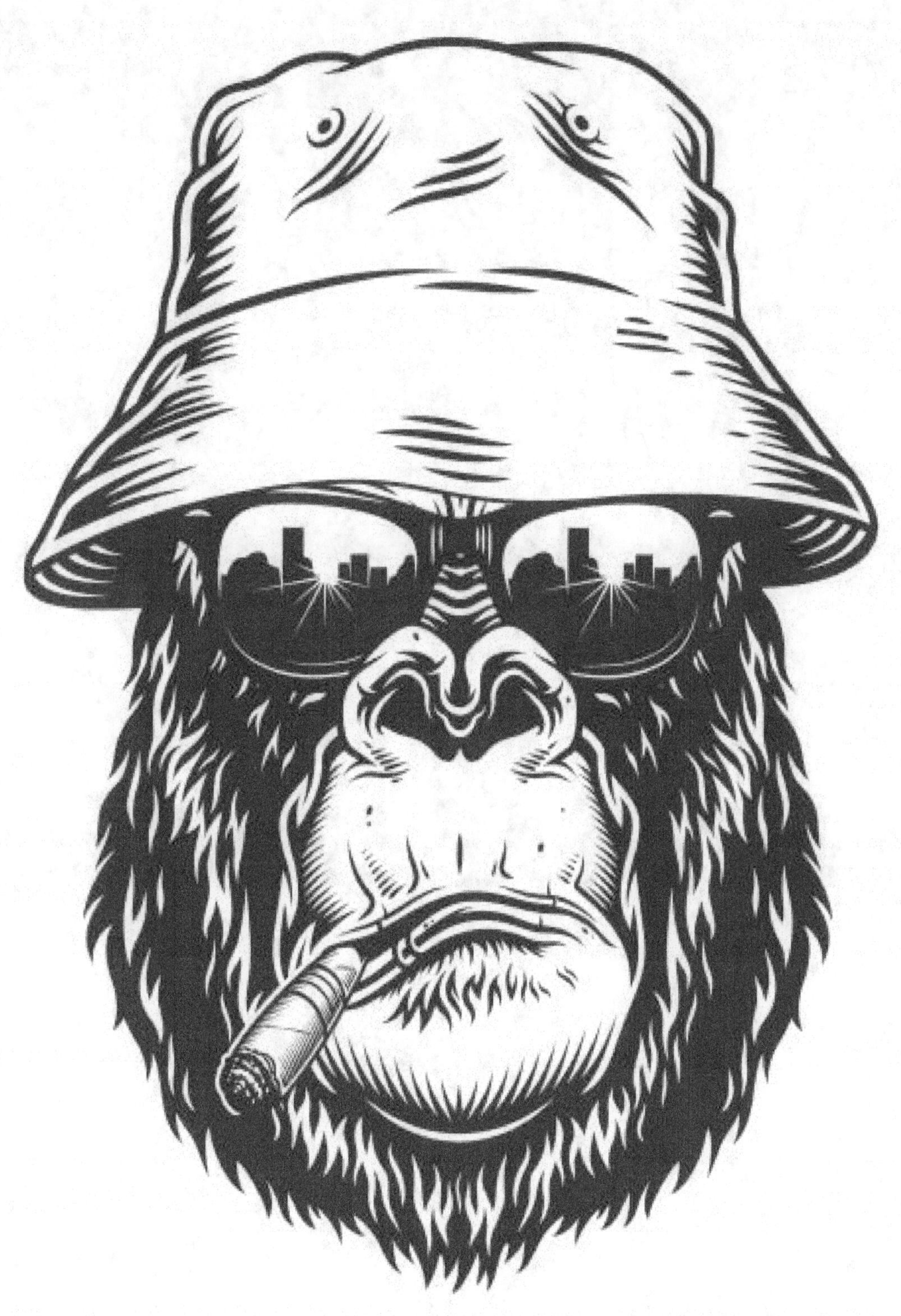

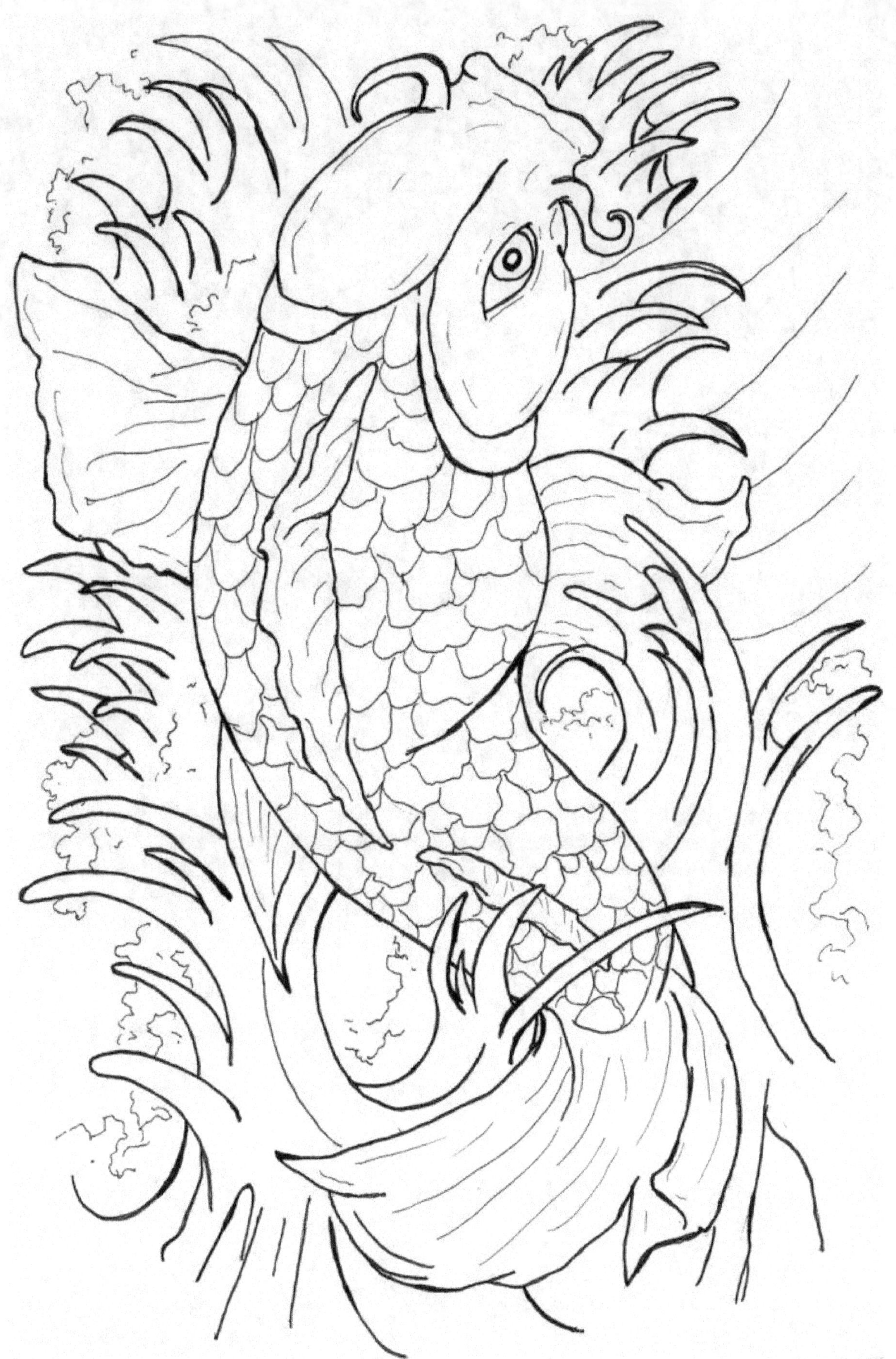

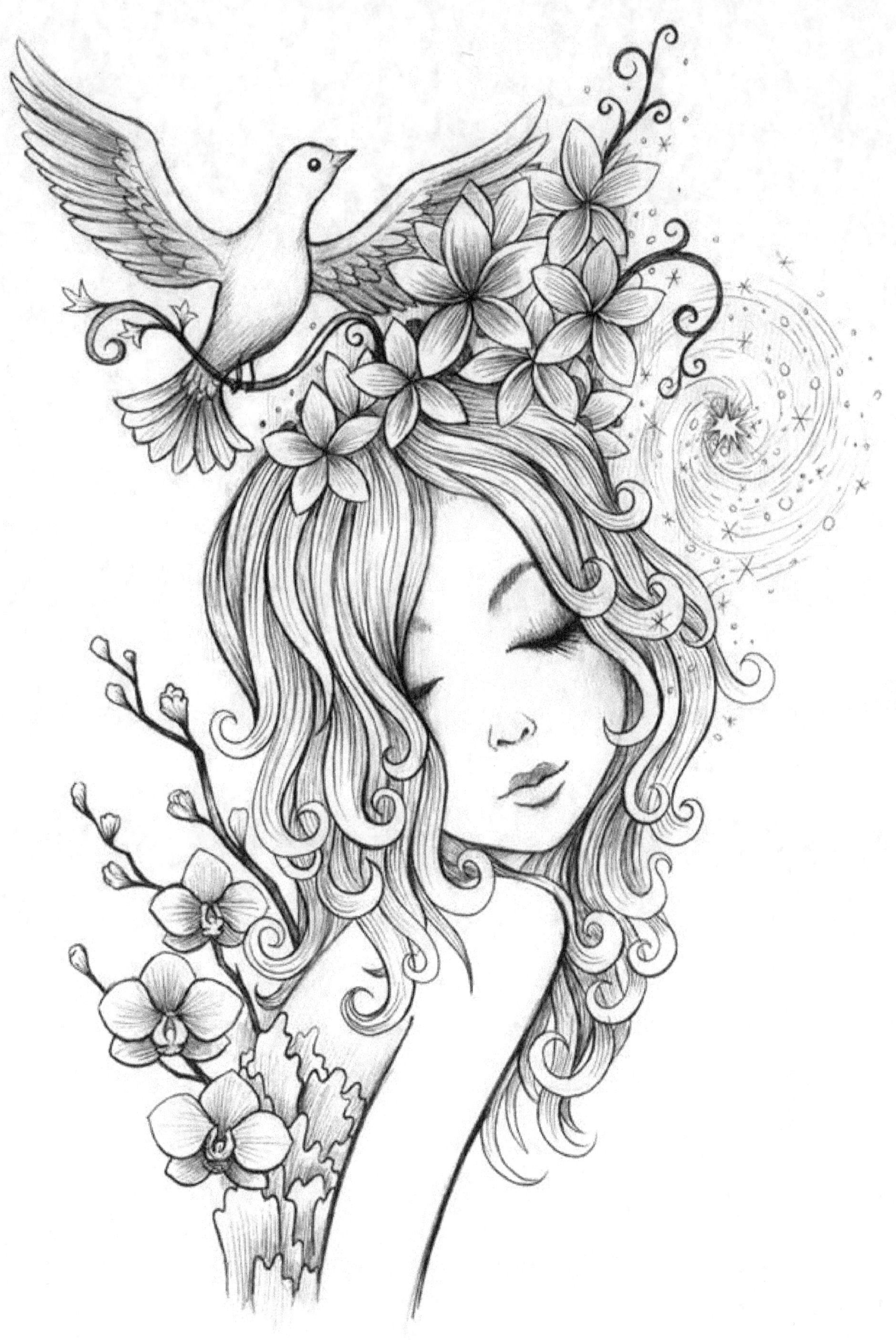

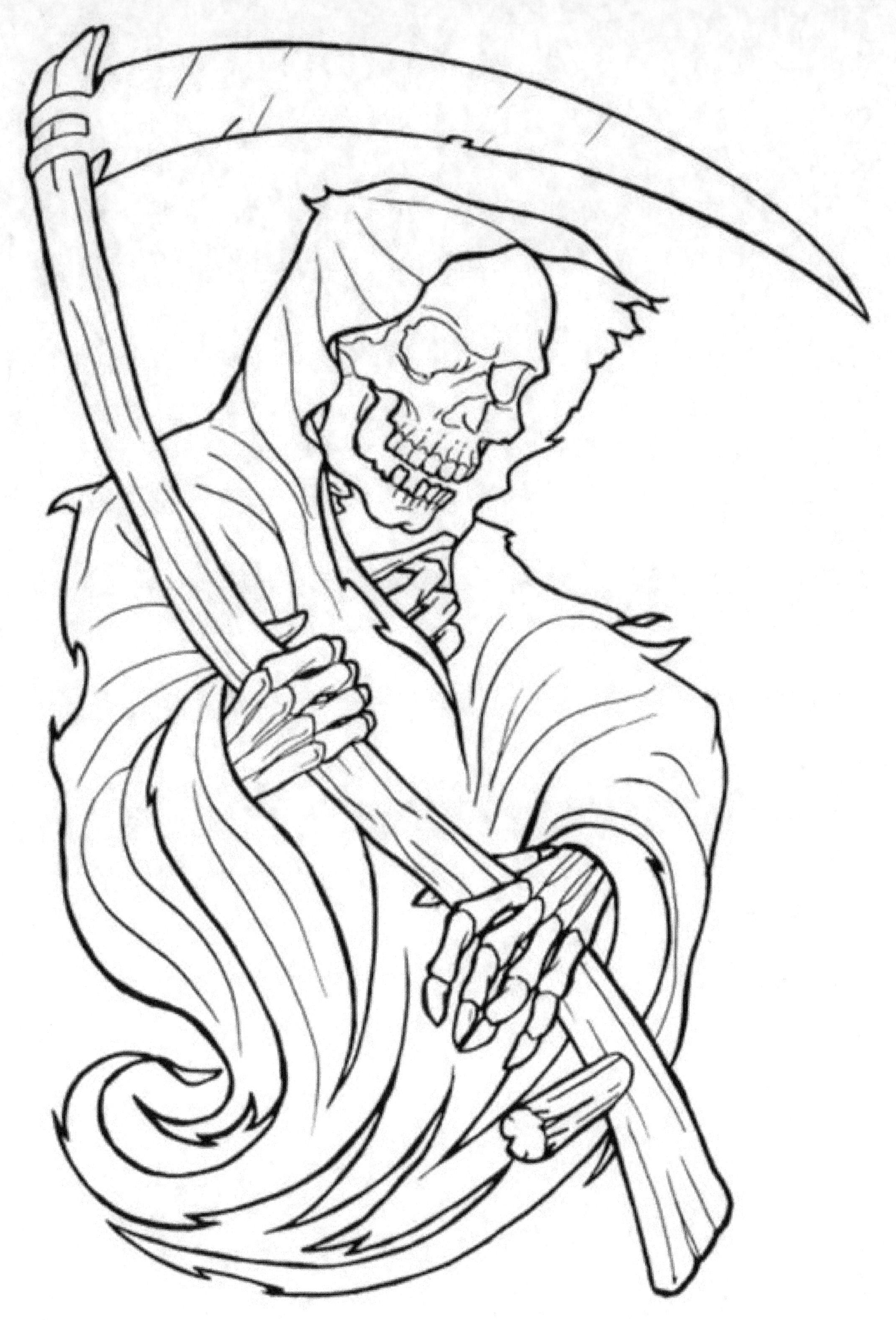

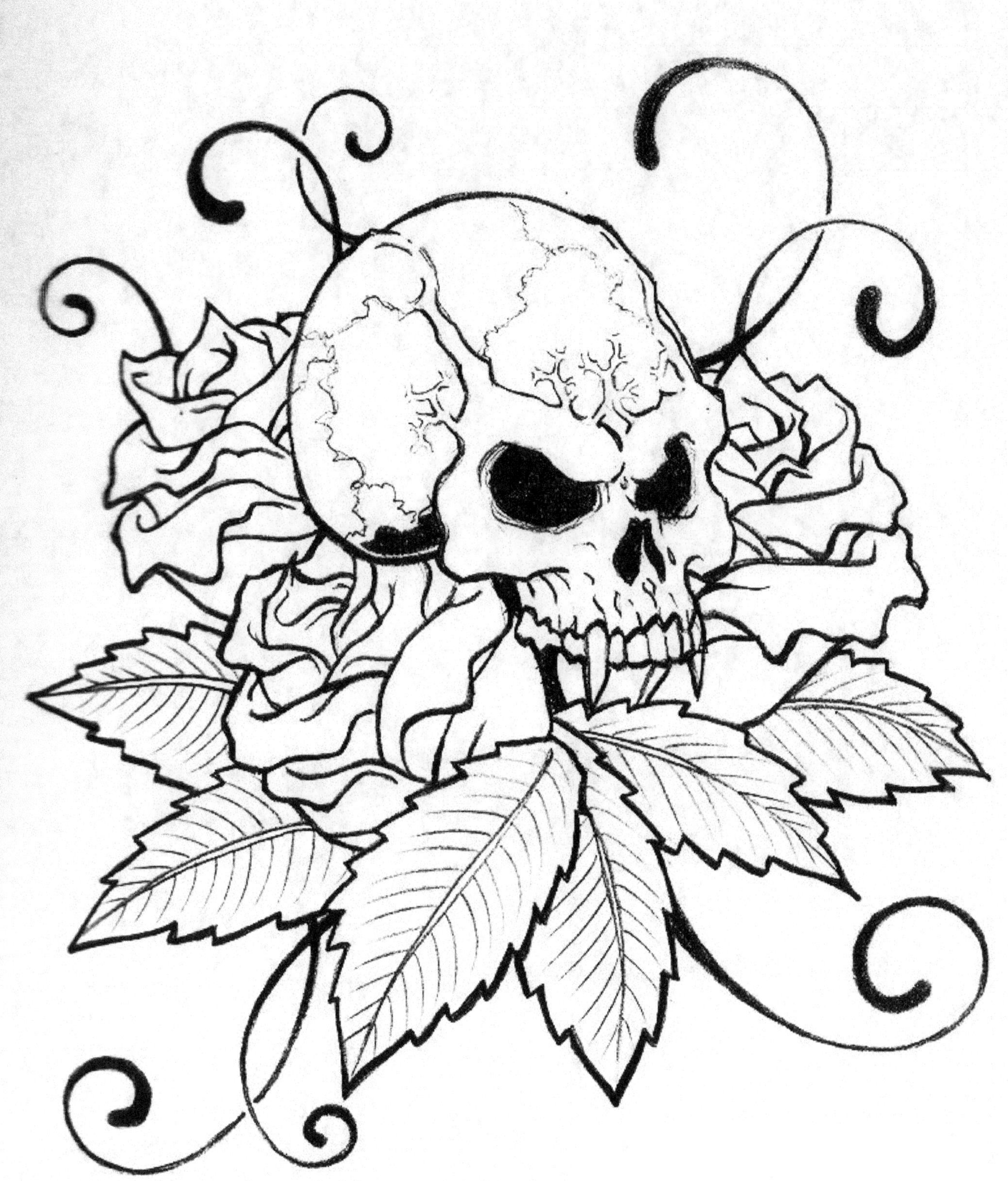

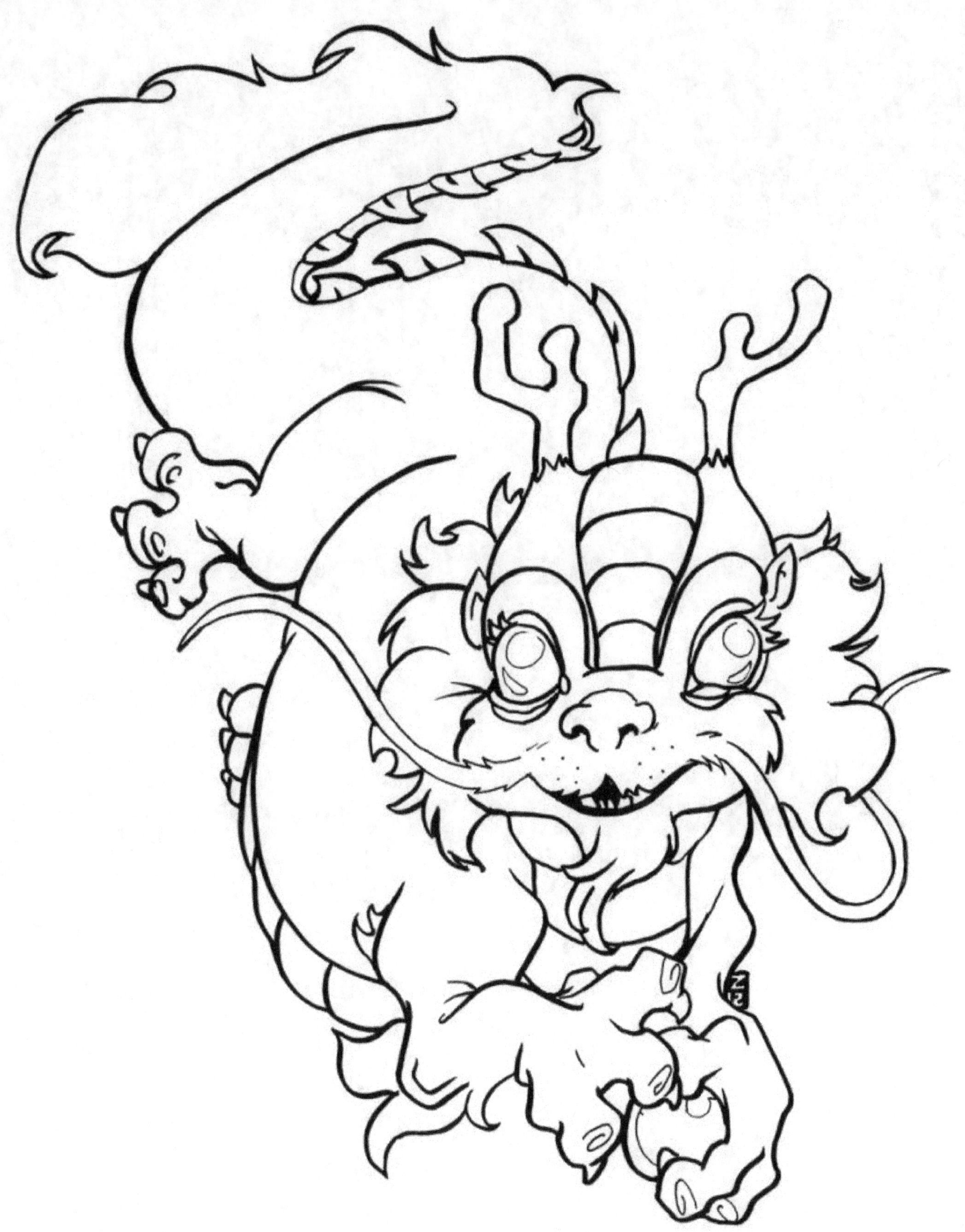

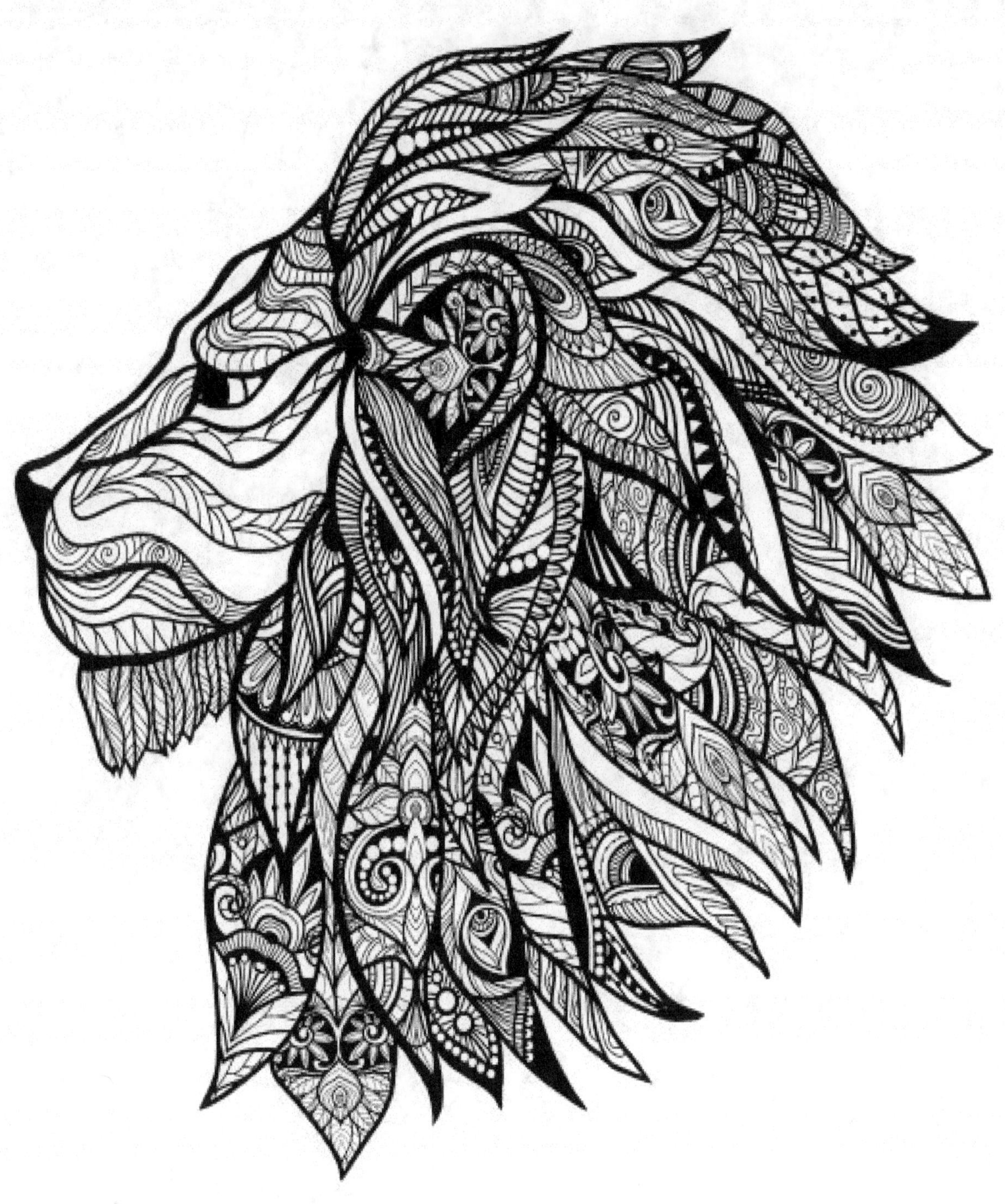

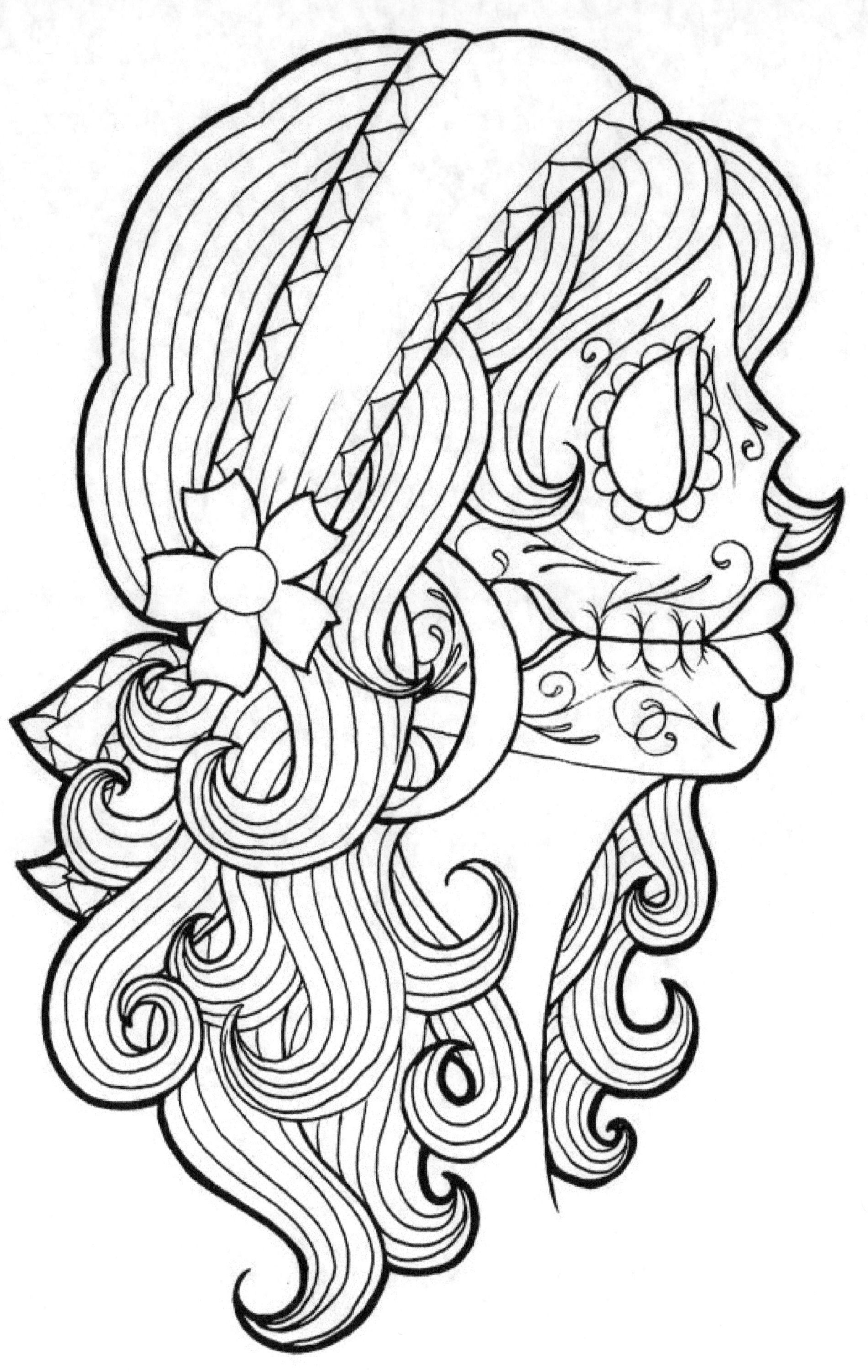

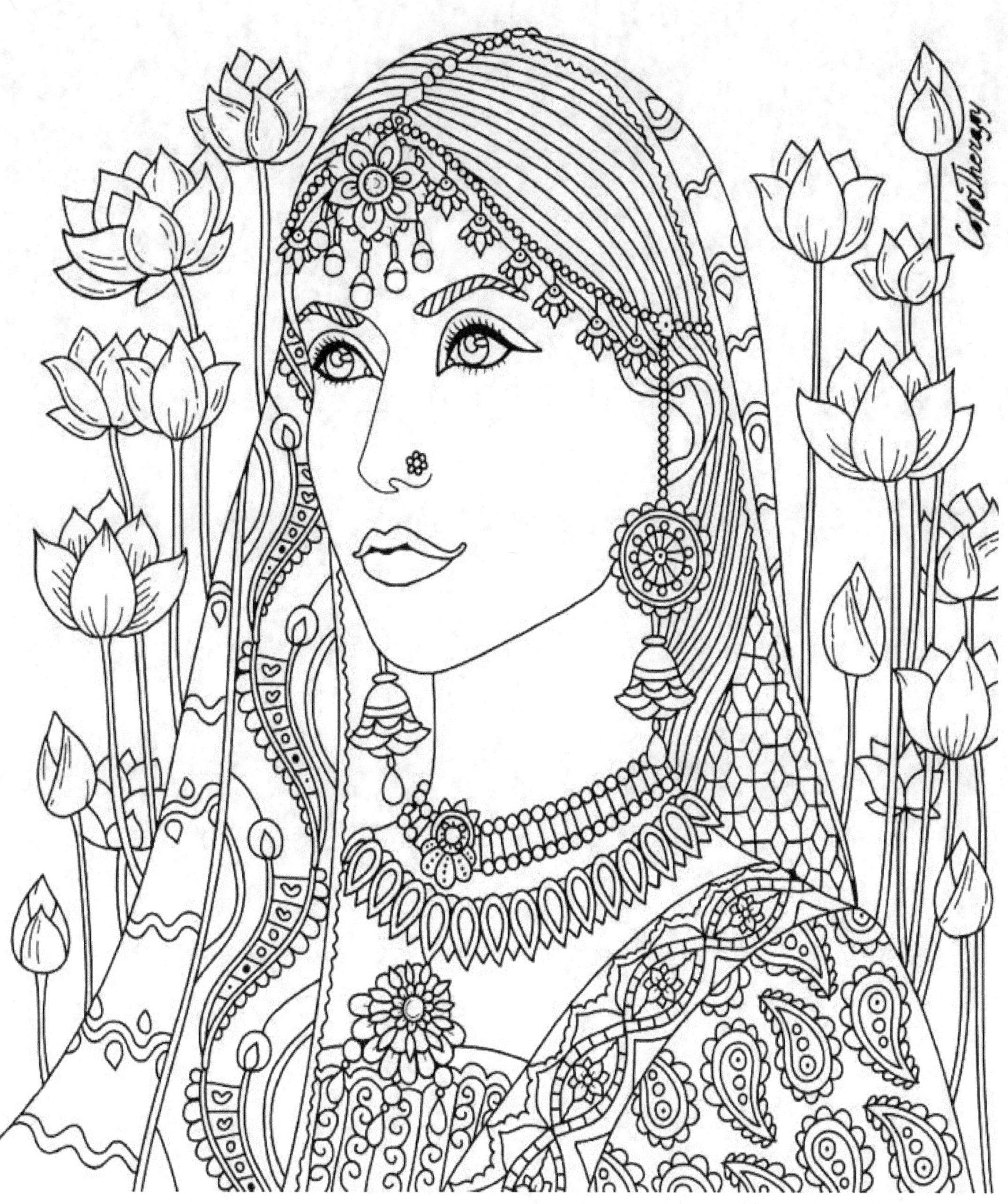
ColorTherapy

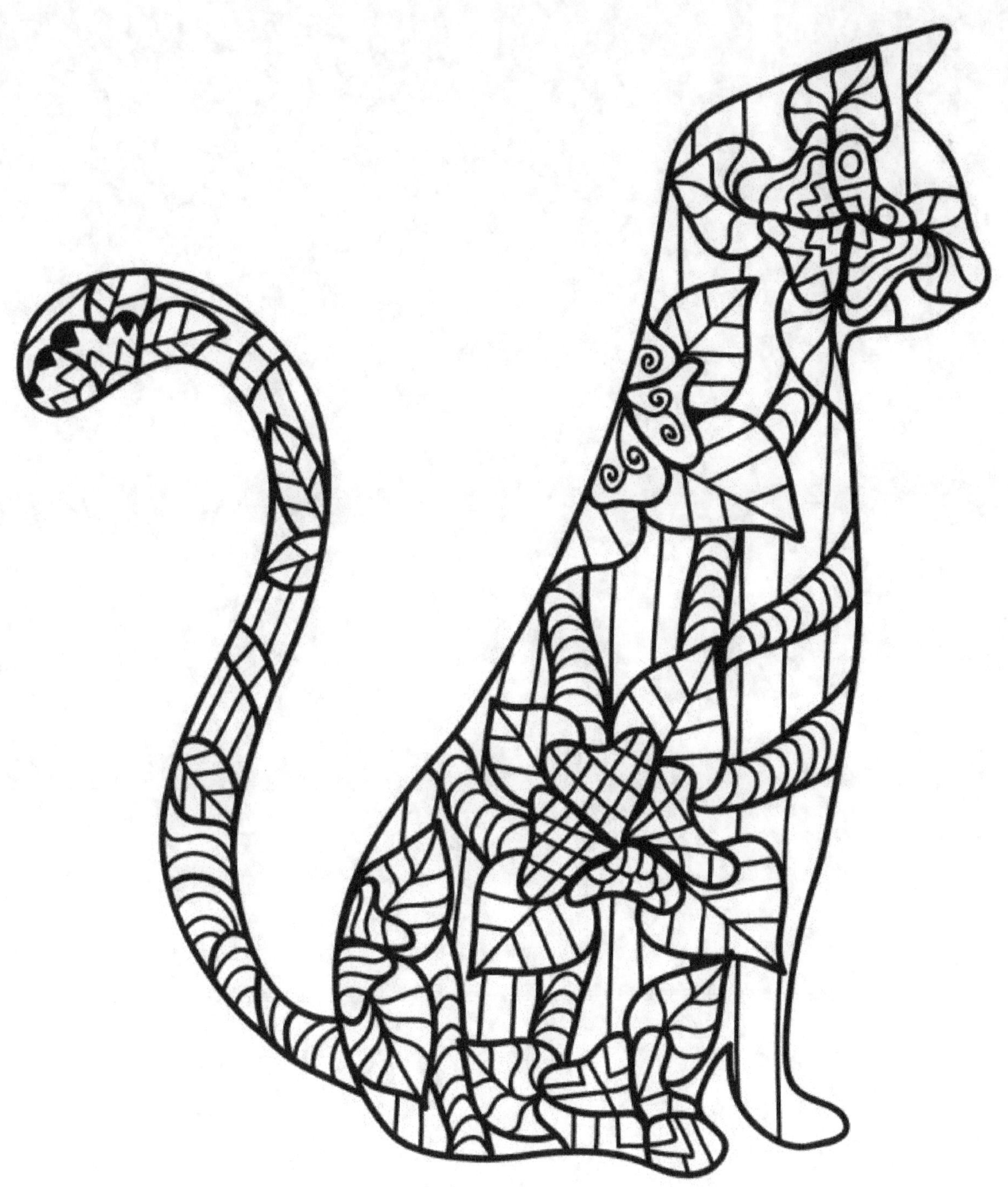

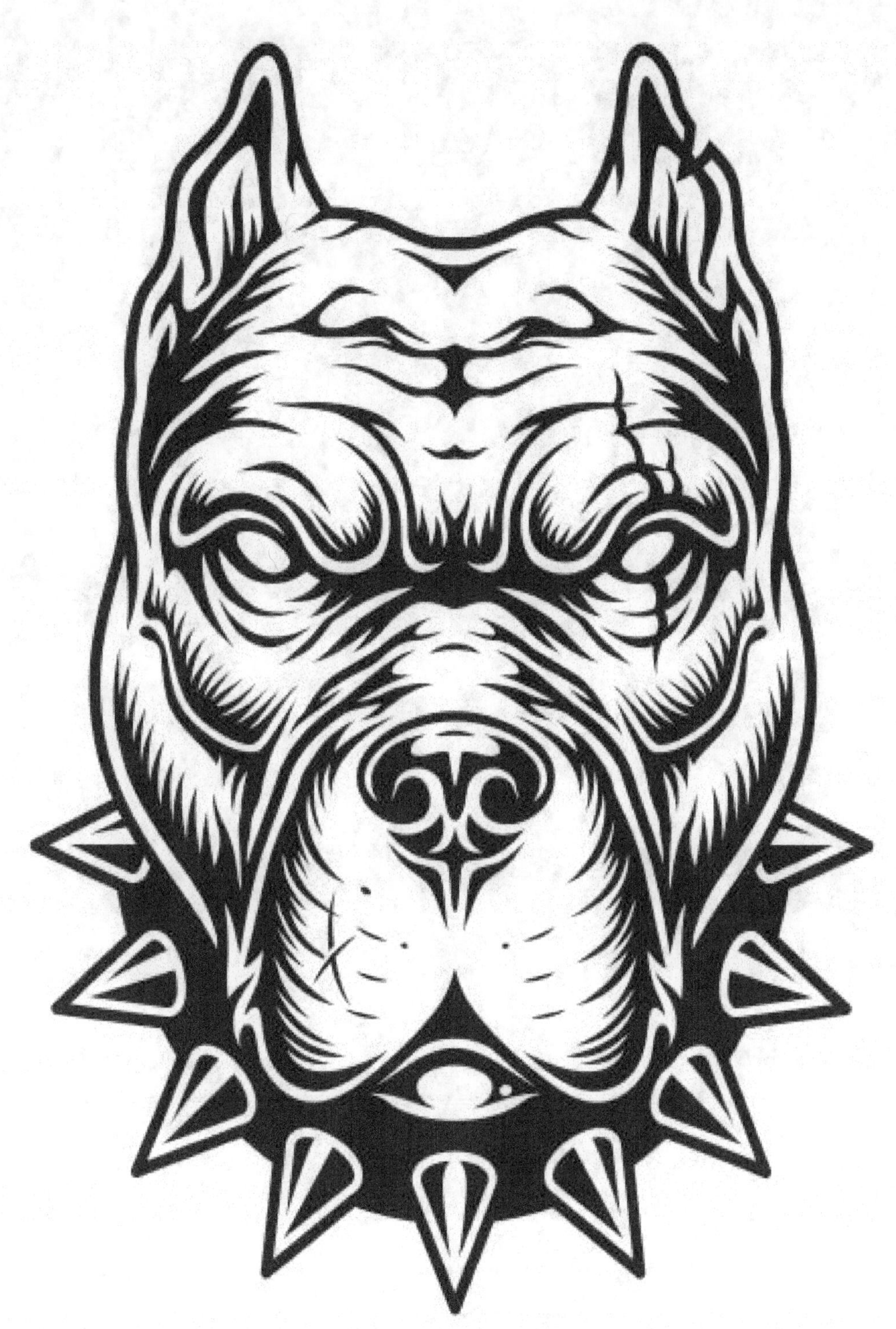

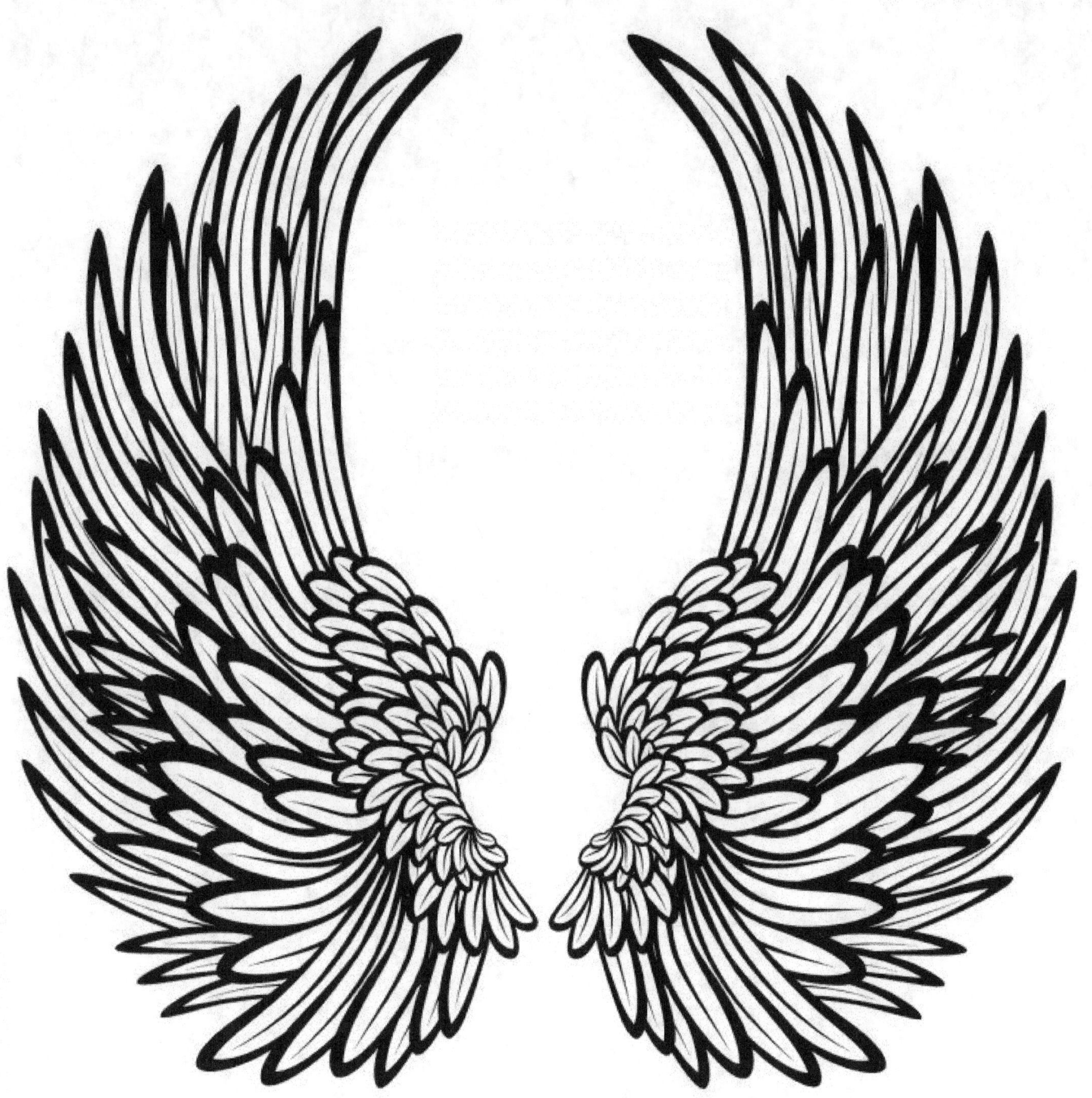

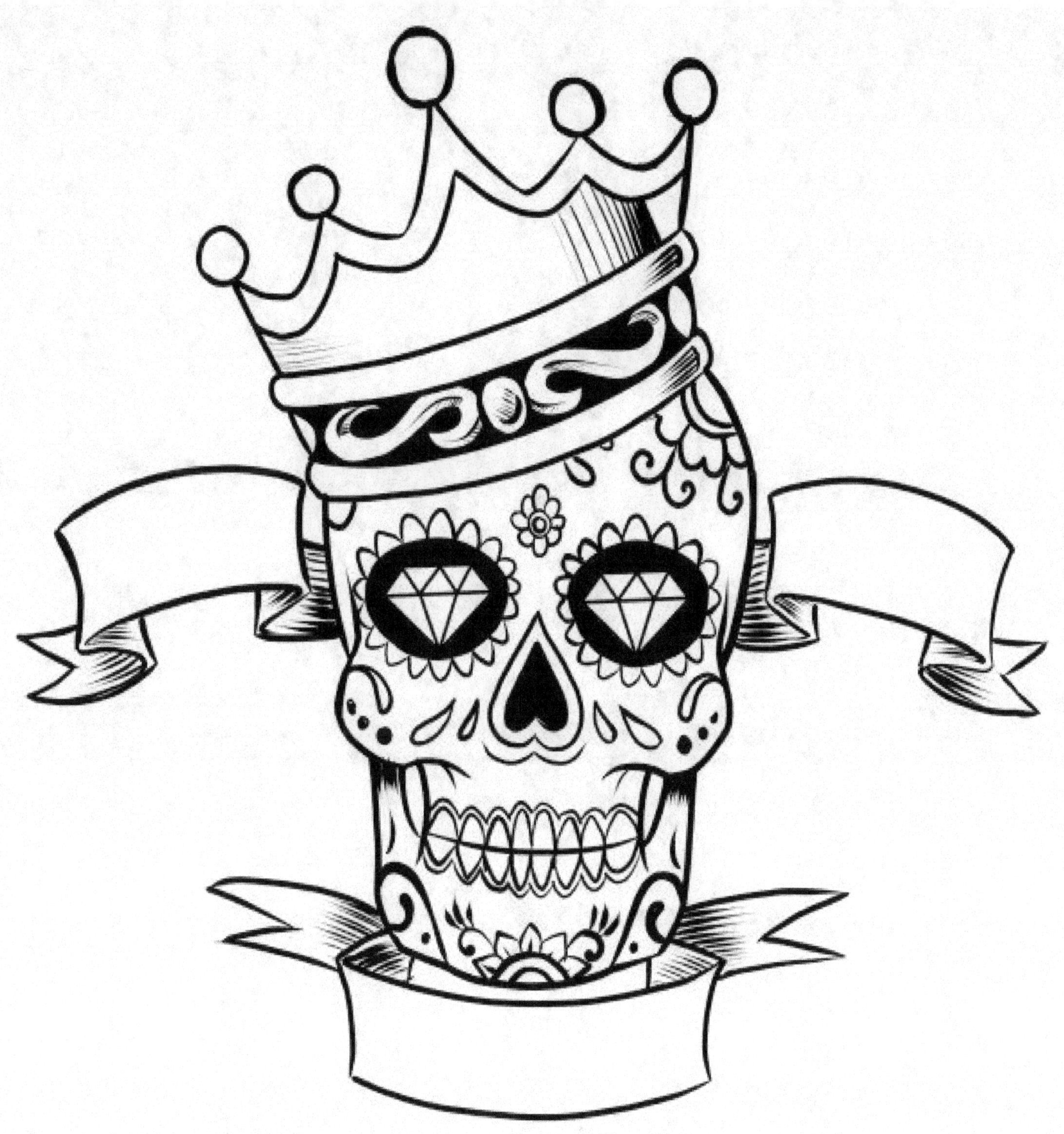

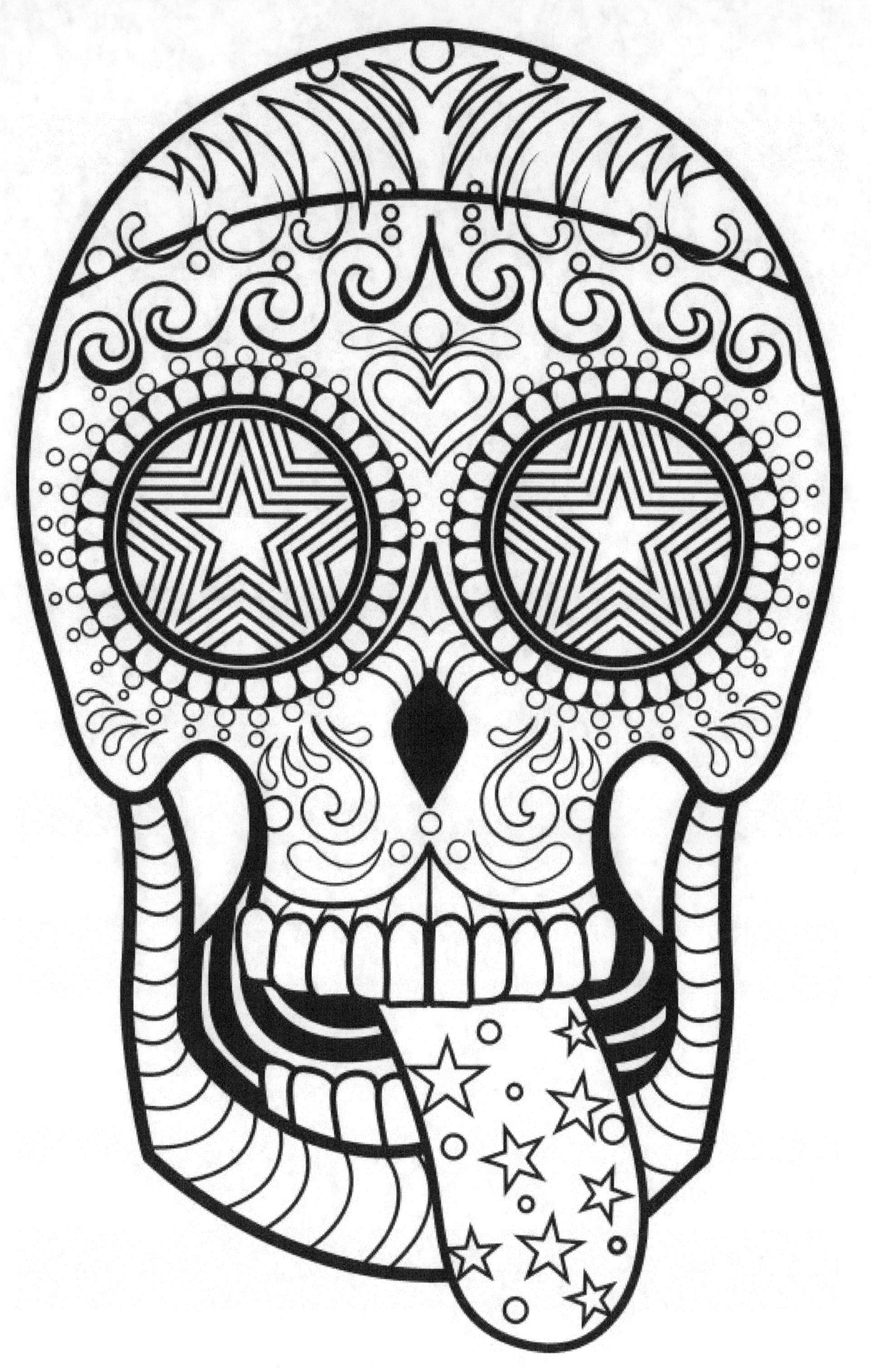

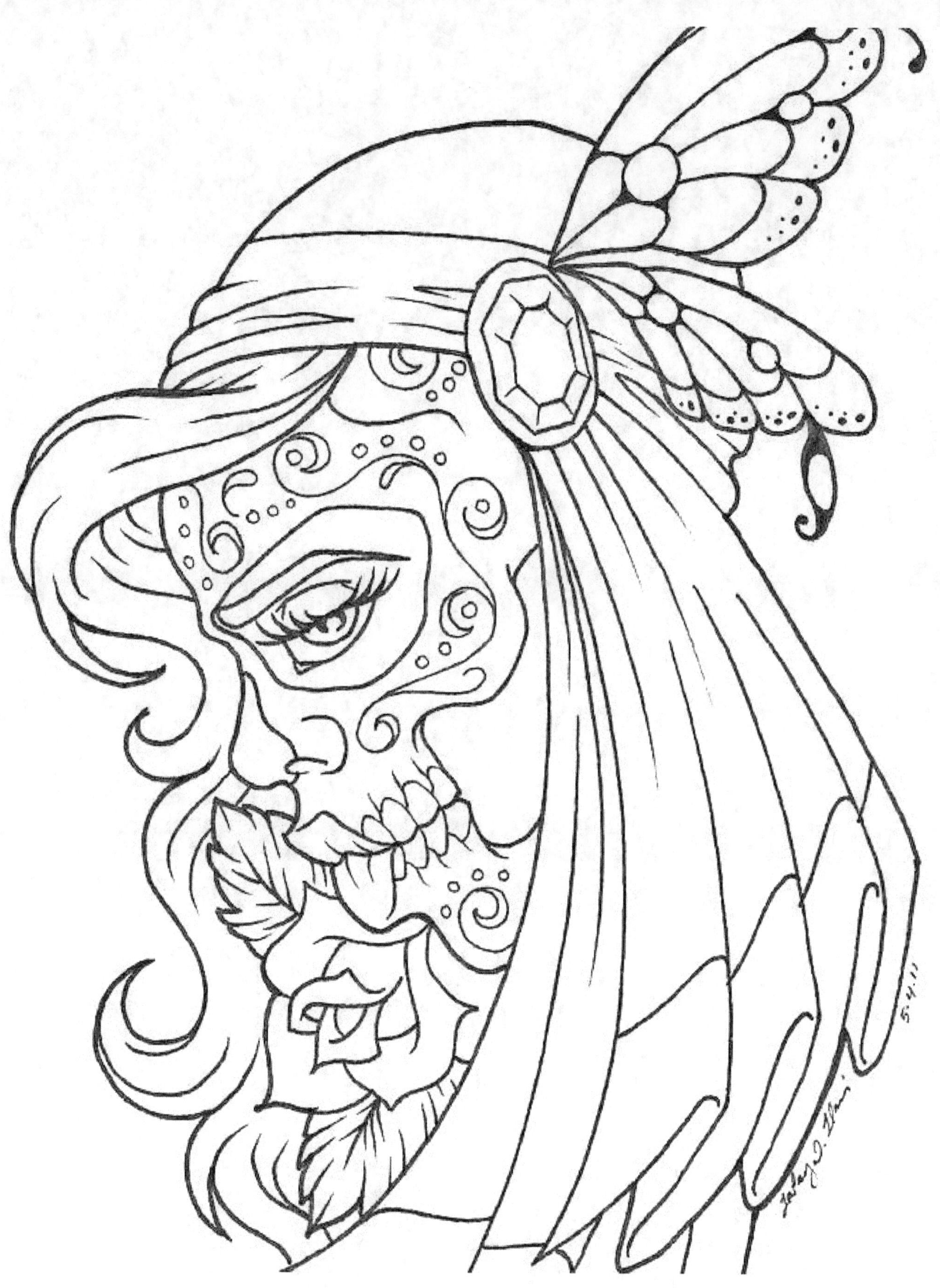

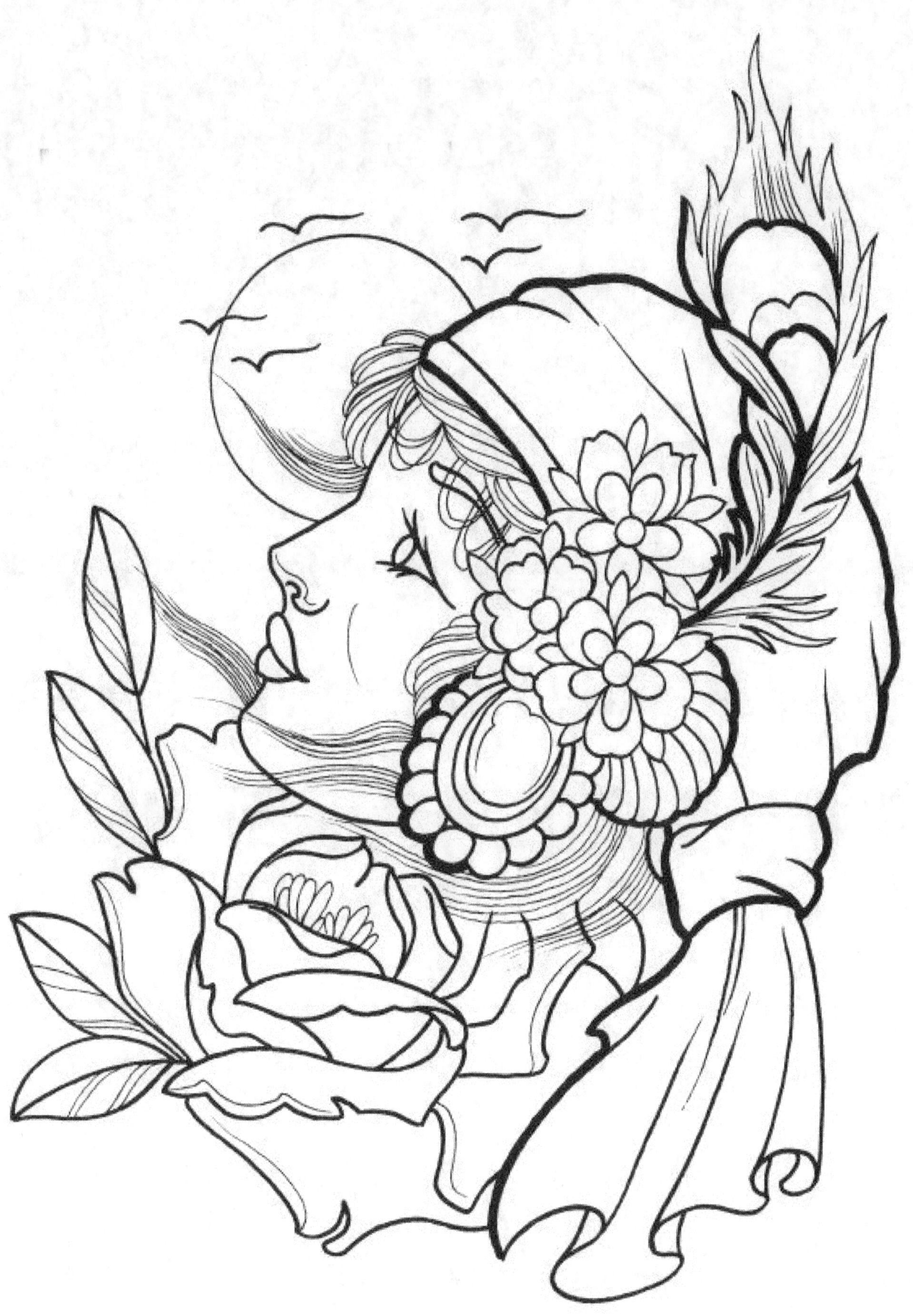

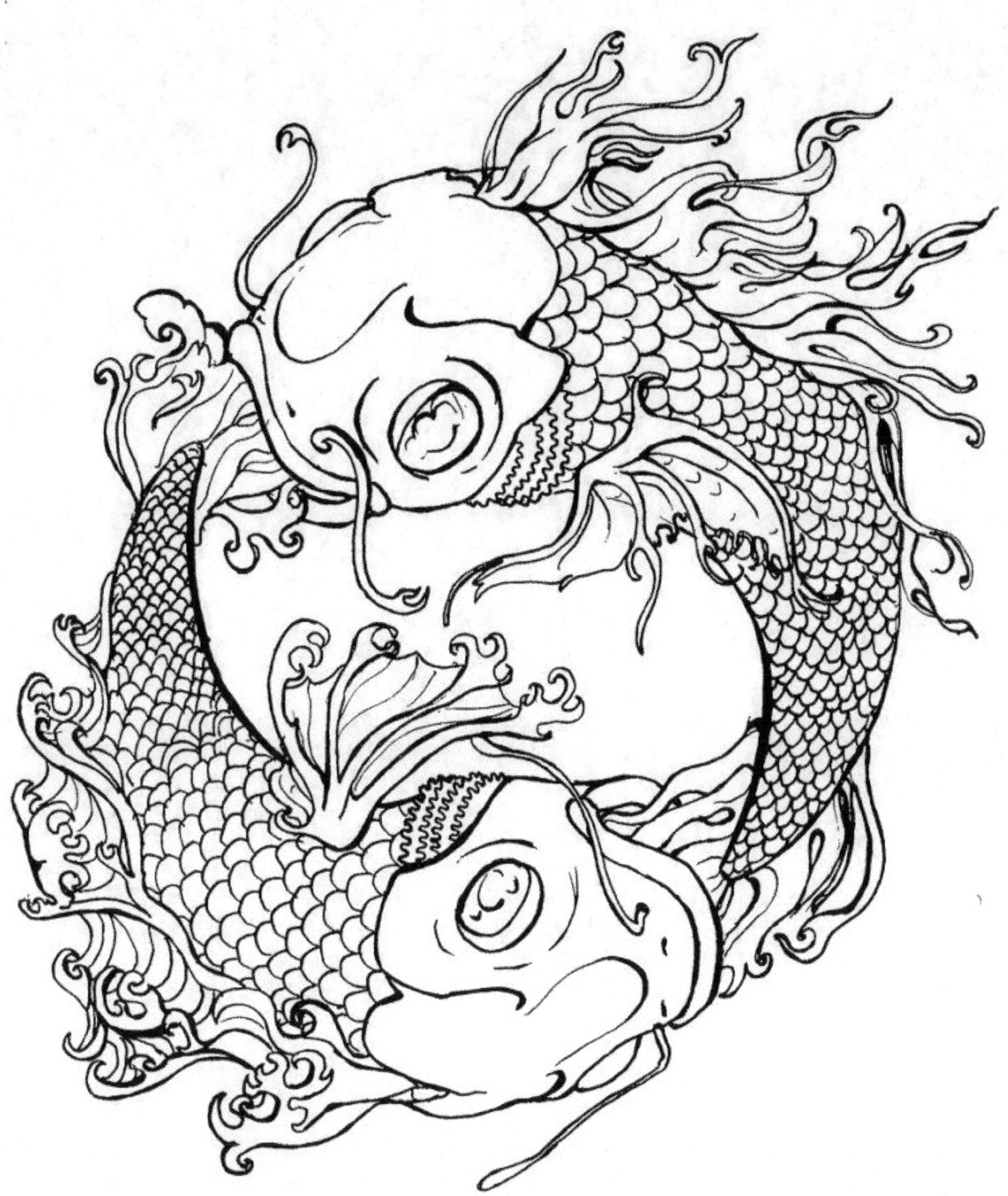